JAPAN AND AMERICA

Japan and America

From Earliest Times to the Present

LAWRENCE H. *enry* BATTISTINI

With five maps

GREENWOOD PRESS, PUBLISHERS
WESTPORT, CONNECTICUT

To my brother, ALFRED

PREFACE

This book is intended to be an introduction to the history of Japanese-American relations from their origins in the nineteenth century to the present time. The emphasis is on the political phase of these relations. The book is based on a study of the numerous works which have appeared on the subject, together with a critical examination of pertinent documents and other primary materials. The book does not purport to make any novel or sensational disclosures. It aims to re-examine and re-evaluate the facts from the standpoint of the contemporary positions and problems of the United States and Japan.

The book is written in the layman's language and stress is placed on the main threads of developments rather than details. Footnotes are kept to a minimum and are largely in the nature of acknowledgments for the research and judgments of others. I felt it necessary to document Chapter VI extensively, however, because of its still controversial nature. Diacritical marks are not employed in the spellings of Asiatic names in the text, since the general reader is probably not interested in, or familiar with, them. Long-vowel marks are used on Japanese names appearing in the appendices, however. This is done because those readers who may be interested in the appendices probably desire the exact pronunciation of the Japanese names.

It is hoped that in addition to serving as a concise account for the general reader, and as an introduction for the prospective student of the subject, the book may have some usefulness in contributing toward a sound and more diffused understanding of Japanese-American relations and problems.

I wish to thank A. J. Miller, S. J., Dean of the International Division, Sophia University (Tokyo), for the many courtesies extended during the preparation of this book; Mr. David W. Heron, Librarian of the American Embassy in Tokyo, for facilitating the use of the Embassy Library; and certain officials of the Japanese Foreign Office, for having checked the accuracy of various data. Gratitude is expressed to the following for having generously given of their personal time; Miss Midori Yamanouchi, for typing, research and other valued assistance; Miss Eri Sakai, for typing and helpful editorial suggestions; and Miss Shigeko Sheila Yamamoto, for assistance in proof reading. I also wish to thank the John Day Company for their kind permission to use three maps which appeared in my *Introducing Asia*.

Tokyo

—L.H.B.

CONTENTS

JAPAN AND AMERICA

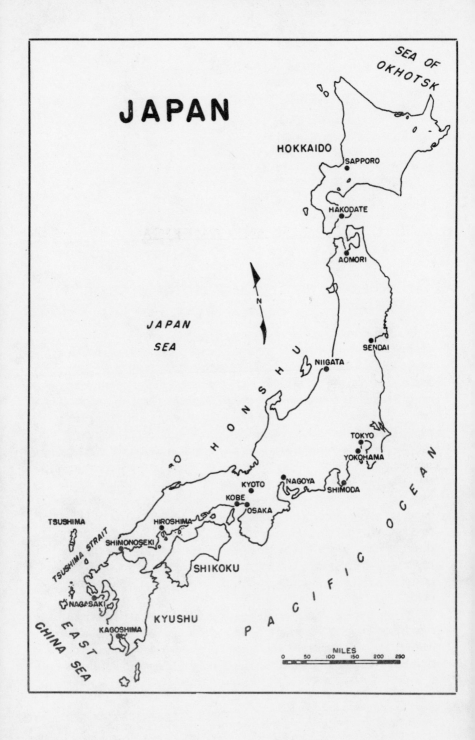

CHAPTER I

THE ESTABLISHMENT OF TREATY RELATIONS

JAPAN'S EARLY RELATIONS WITH THE OUTSIDE WORLD

Japan did not become exposed to the West until the sixteenth century. Prior to then the Japanese had led a somewhat secluded existence and the principal outside contacts had been with Korea and China. Contacts with Korea were established in the early centuries of the Christian era, when Koreans came to Japan as teachers, artisans and merchants. Since the Koreans were exponents of the very advanced Chinese culture of that time, the Japanese accordingly caught their first glimpse of a vastly superior civilization. From the eighth to the tenth centuries the Japanese were in direct contact with China. Some trade was carried on, and considerable numbers of Chinese came to Japan to serve as teachers while large numbers of Japanese went to China for study and observation. After the tenth century direct contacts with China diminished, but the dynamic impact of Chinese culture had had its potent influence and in effect had transformed the traditional culture of Japan into a semi-Chinese culture pattern of a high order.

The contact of Japan with Korea and China was historically significant primarily because of the profound cultural effect it had on Japan. Politically the contacts resulted in no particularly significant developments, although Kublai Khan did unsuccessfully attempt to invade and subjugate Japan in the latter part of the thirteenth century, and the Japanese for their part attempted to establish some political control over Korea. In the latter part of the sixteenth century the Japanese dictator Hideyoshi invaded Korea with huge armies as the preliminary move of an attempt to subjugate the decadent China of the Mings. In the end, the armies of Hideyoshi were compelled to evacuate Korea and return to Japan, but only after they had inflicted great cruelties on the Koreans, leaving behind a legacy of hatred which putatively endured for generations.

In addition to the cultural and commercial contacts with Korea and China, the Japanese also carried on a seafaring trade with various areas of Southeast Asia. These trading activities were generally sporadic, however, and of very little political or even cultural significance.

JAPAN'S FIRST CONTACTS WITH THE WEST

The West's earliest contacts with Japan were largely a consequence of the Renaissance and its outgrowth of mercantilism and missionary zeal. It was therefore the West rather than Japan which bridged the great gap between the two. Westerners began arriving in Japan in the sixteenth century, principally to promote trade and to gain converts for Christianity. The first Westerners to reach the shores of Japan were Portuguese, who arrived in 1541, followed by Spaniards, the Dutch, and then the English. The Dutch and English came primarily for trade, whereas the Portuguese and Spaniards were chiefly interested in the promotion of Christianity, although trade motives were also a factor. Following the arrival of the Jesuit, St. Francis Xavier, in 1549, Christianity made notable progress, and by the end of the century the number of Christians in Japan came to number some 300,000. For various reasons, however, the missionaries became subjected to severe persecutions during the latter part of the century. Under Iemitsu, who was Shogun from 1622 to 1661, all Westerners, except a stipulated few, were expelled from Japan and Christianity was practically exterminated. Thousands of Japanese Christians were tortured and killed, and the profession of Christianity by any Japanese became a crime punishable by death. As a result, most surviving Japanese Christians abandoned their new faith, but a not inconsiderable number on the island of Kyushu clandestinely clung to the faith until religious toleration was promulgated in the latter part of the nineteenth century.

THE TOKUGAWA SECLUSION-EXCLUSION PERIOD

Early in the seventeenth century the Tokugawa clan consolidated its power in Japan by force of arms and established an iron rule over the country which endured until the overthrow of the Tokugawas and the " restoration " of the Emperor in 1868. During this relatively long period of more than two and a half centuries Japan functioned under a dual system of government. Under this dual system, actual power was firmly concentrated in the hands of the Tokugawas, who ruled effectively by means of a so-called Shogunate system, with its capital in Edo (now known as Tokyo). Nominal power remained in the hands of the do-nothing emperor, residing in the ancient capital of Kyoto, who in effect remained only the symbol of divine authority and in whose name the Shogun allegedly ruled.

During the Tokugawa period Japan was committed to a policy of seclusion and exclusion which attempted to isolate the country from the rest of the world. This policy made it a criminal offense for any Japanese to leave the country for any purpose whatsoever, and any Japanese who escaped from the country and then attempted to reenter were subject to summary execution. Even the reading of foreign books was strictly forbidden.* Foreigners, in turn, were forbidden to enter any part of Japan, and even shipwrecked

---

* This restriction was considerably relaxed by the beginning of the nineteenth century. By the third and fourth decades of that century there were many evidences of the inevitable breakdown of the seclusion-exclusion policy.

foreign sailors were prohibited from seeking haven on Japanese soil. The only foreigners permitted in Japan were a limited number of Dutch and Chinese who were authorized to carry on restricted commercial operations from prescribed bases in the Nagasaki area. During this long period of seclusion-exclusion, the Dutch exercised an extra-commercial function of significant value to the Tokugawas, namely that of a " window," so to speak, from which information came concerning the outside world. It was from the Dutch (as well as from the Chinese), for example, that the Tokugawas learned of the European aggressions in China in the early nineteenth century, and particularly of the notorious Opium War between China and Great Britain.

EARLY AMERICAN CONTACTS WITH JAPAN

It is possible that an American ship may have entered Japanese waters as early as 1790, but nothing is known of its identity or the details concerning its visitation. The " first " American vessels therefore may have been the *Lady Washington* and the *Grace*, which appeared off the southern coast of Japan in May 1791.[1] These vessels were on their way to China and attempted, in Japan to dispose of some sea otter pelts.[2] The next known American ship to enter Japanese waters was the *Eliza*, commanded by Captain Stewart, which arrived in 1797. This ship was actually chartered by the Dutch, whose commercial intercourse with Japan was temporarily suspended as a result of the Netherlands' involvement in war with Great Britain. During the period of this war several other American vessels in the service of the Dutch also called at Nagasaki on commercial missions. In 1810 Captain Stewart, on his own account, attempted to unload a cargo at Nagasaki, but he was peremptorily rebuffed by the Shogun's officials who curtly reminded him of the law forbidding intercourse with any foreigners except the Dutch and Chinese. He tried again in 1813 to unload another cargo, but again without success. Between 1791 and 1807 some fourteen American ships are definitely known to have visited Japan on thirteen different occasions. Nine of these vessels were chartered by the Dutch between 1797 and 1807. The five other ships made unsuccessful private attempts to carry on trade. Between 1807 and 1837 no American vessels are known to have entered Japanese waters, although during this period John Quincy Adams, as President of the United States, saw fit to declare it to be " the right and even the duty of Christian nations to open the ports of Japan, and the duty of Japan to assent, on the ground that no nation has the right," any more than any man, to withdraw " its private contribution to the welfare of the world." In 1837 the *Morrison*, flying the stars and stripes, entered Japanese waters and was also denied permission to put in at any port. Not until 1845 did another American vessel enter Japanese waters, but between that year and 1849 at least twelve American ships entered Japanese seas, although none of them accomplished their missions.[3]

To return to the *Morrison*. The trip of the *Morrison* to Japan was the idea of Charles W. King, a young partner of Olyphant and Company, one of the leading foreign trading firms in China. King aimed to combine humanitarianism and idealism with practical objectives. In Canton he took on board seven Japanese nationals who had been shipwrecked and assembled at that port for return to Japan. He hoped that the officials of the Japanese Government would be grateful for the return of these nationals and that commercial relations of some kind might consequently be negotiated. He also hoped to be instrumental in opening Japan to missionary activity. The *Morrison* entered Edo Bay in July 1837 and anchored off Uraga. Although the vessel was unarmed and carried no Christian literature (whose circulation was forbidden in Japan at that time), it received a very hostile reception. It was fired upon by the Edo forts and was compelled to withdraw to Kagoshima, where it was again fired upon. The mission ended in complete failure. None of the Japanese nationals were disembarked and the vessel returned to Canton.[4]

In 1845 another effort was made by an American vessel to enter

Edo Bay when the captain of the *Manhattan* sought to discharge eleven shipwrecked Japanese who had been rescued from a barren Pacific island. In this instance, however, the captain of the vessel was permitted to deliver the Japanese, and in appreciation was allowed to linger in the bay for four days, after which he was compelled to sail his vessel out of Japanese waters.

Meanwhile, in 1835, a Mr. Edmund Roberts had departed from Washington with a letter written by President Jackson for the Emperor of Japan, transcribed in Latin and Dutch. Roberts had been instructed to land at some port other than Nagasaki to preclude any obstructionist tactics on the part of the Dutch, whom the Americans believed to be jealous of their exclusive trading privileges and in the habit of exposing plans of other nations and nationals to the Shogunate. Roberts carried appropriate presents with him and was authorized to promise the Japanese additional presents amounting to as much as $10,000 in return for a treaty arrangement between Japan and America. En route, however, Roberts died in Macao and hence was unable to complete his mission.

By the 1840's a considerable number of American sailing vessels were frequenting Japanese waters. Some of the vessels passed through these waters on their way to Canton, the entrepôt of the China trade, while others were engaged in the extensive whaling operations of that period in the North Pacific. American vessels were frequently wrecked by storms and the crews were often forced to seek refuge on Japanese shores. Since shipwrecked sailors, regardless of their ill luck, were regarded as violating the fundamental law of Japan, they were generally roughly handled and often subjected to cruel treatment.

Partly because of concern for the China trade which made Japan highly desirable as a port of call for revictualizing and taking on other supplies, and partly because of humanitarian concern for the welfare of shipwrecked American sailors who might be forced to seek haven on Japanese soil, the Congress became keenly interested in concluding a treaty arrangement with

Japan. In 1845 Representative Zedoc Pratt of New York introduced a resolution in the House of Representatives which called for the immediate negotiation of a treaty with Japan. Actually, commerce was the primary motive of this resolution, which stated that " the day and hour have now arrived for turning the enterprise of our merchants and seamen into the harbors and markets of those long secluded countries."[5]

In implementation of this resolution, Commodore Biddle, who was then stationed in China, was instructed to proceed to Japan and exert his utmost efforts toward concluding a treaty of commerce and amity. Acting on his instructions, Biddle arrived in Edo Bay on July 20, 1846, and was immediately surrounded by a considerable number of hostile Japanese craft. His overtures for a treaty were met with procrastination and even rudeness, and seven days after his arrival in the bay he was curtly instructed to withdraw to Nagasaki and further informed that no treaty was possible under any circumstances. During the discussions Biddle was either pushed or struck by a samurai and his failure to retaliate, while an act of magnanimity on his part, is alleged to have caused him to lose the respect of the Japanese. At any rate, the Biddle mission ended in complete failure, and he withdrew from Japanese waters.

In 1846 Dr. Peter Parker, in charge of the American legation in Peking, informed the Secretary of State that the survivors of the American whaler *Lawrence* had been imprisoned by the Japanese and treated with undue harshness. Commodore Glynn was thereupon instructed to proceed to Japan for the rescue of the shipwrecked and imprisoned nationals. In command of the *Preble* he reached Nagasaki in 1849 and actually succeeded in securing the release of the imprisoned Americans, whom he returned to Canton.[6] The rescued Americans confirmed the reports of the cruel treatment they had received at the hands of the Japanese. In 1849 survivors from the American whaler *Trident*, which had been wrecked near one of the Kurile Islands, were also rescued through the assistance of the Dutch.[7]

THE FIRST PERRY VISIT

The discovery of gold in California in 1848 and the subsequent rapid settlement of the Pacific Coast resulted in a greatly increased American interest in the Far East. Moreover, whaling operations at this time had reached peak activity. In 1850, for example, a Japanese official counted 86 American ships that passed in view from a single point in Japan. The problem of a treaty with Japan consequently became increasingly urgent, and it was even discussed on the cabinet level. Finally, in June 1851, President Fillmore commissioned Commodore Aulick to negotiate a treaty with Japan which would relax the existing severe restrictions on trade and also contain safeguards for the protection of shipwrecked American sailors seeking haven in Japan. Aulick, then in command of the East India squadron, sailed for Canton in July of that year. On his arrival there he was informed that his commission had been withdrawn. Among other reasons for the withdrawal of his commission, Washington had apparently given sober second thought to the rigid qualifications required of a man heading such an important mission, and it was decided that Matthew Calbraith Perry, because of his background and temperament, was much better suited for the historic assignment.

In connection with Perry's expedition and its relation to America's expanding interests in the vast Pacific area, it is of interest to note the vision of William Seward, the Secretary of State during the Civil War. In 1852 when he was a member of the Senate, Seward had opined that the Atlantic interests of the United States would " relatively sink in importance, while the Pacific Ocean, its islands, and the vast regions beyond" would become " the chief theatre of events in the world's great hereafter." Seward further expressed the belief that the commercial interests of the United States in the Pacific area would become increasingly important, and that the United States, as the leading Pacific state, was destined to play a principal part in the renovation of the governments and institutions of Asia.[8] While these views were

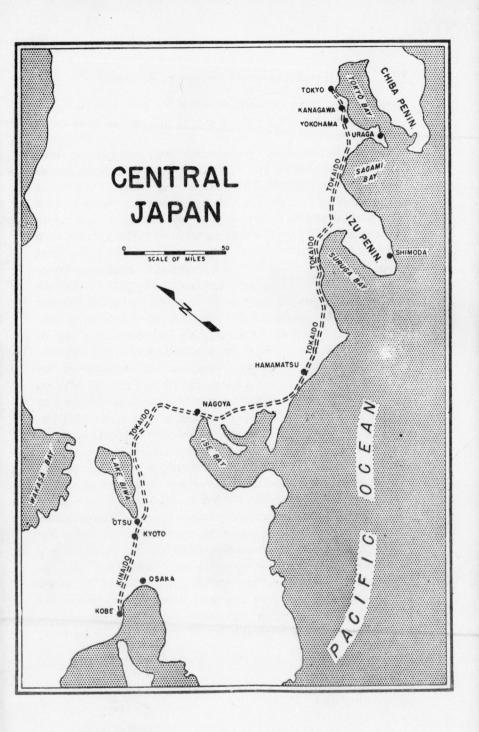

generally considered visionary in their day, it is superfluous to elaborate on how the march of events has proven them to be understatements.

Commodore Perry was given ample time to make the most thorough preparations for his mission, of whose historic importance he was very acutely aware. Navigation charts were purchased from the Dutch, a wide assortment of books on Japan was collected and studied, and even manufacturers were called on for samples of their goods to be taken to Japan with the view of promoting interest in their acquisition.

Perry's instructions were signed by the ad interim Secretary of State, C. M. Conrad. These instructions stipulated that the primary aim of the mission was to secure a treaty containing the following: (1) protection for shipwrecked American sailors, (2) the opening of ports for the refitting and refueling of vessels, and (3) the opening of ports for the conduct of trade. The instructions explicitly urged Perry to be firm in his negotiations but not to resort to the use of force except for self-defense. He was strictly enjoined to forbid his men from engaging in any plundering (a not uncommon avocation of seamen at that time). The instructions noted that: "Recent events—the navigation of the ocean by steam, the acquisition and rapid settlement by this country of a vast territory on the Pacific, the discovery of gold in that region, the rapid communication established across the Isthmus* which separates the two oceans—have practically brought the countries of the east in closer proximity to our own; although the consequences of these events have scarcely begun to be felt, the intercourse between them has already greatly increased and no limits can be assigned to its future expansion." The instructions further urged Perry to bring to the attention of the Japanese the significant fact that Japan and the United States had in effect become neighbors, and that it was up to Japan whether they would be friendly neighbors.[9]

---

* "Isthmus" refers to the Isthmus of Panama, across which a railroad had been constructed.

Perry departed from Norfolk, Virginia, on November 14, 1852, carrying with him a number of gifts and a letter written by President Fillmore for the Emperor of Japan. At Canton Perry took on board Dr. Samuel Wells Williams, to serve as chief interpreter. On July 8, 1853 Perry arrived in Edo Bay, with the decks of all four ships comprising his squadron cleared for action and prepared for any eventuality. Two of the vessels were steamers, the *Susquehanna* and the *Mississippi*, and two were sloops-of-war, the *Saratoga* and the *Plymouth*. The thick black smoke belching from the *Susquehanna* greatly awed the Japanese, and news of the arrival of Perry's " Black Ships " allegedly threw Edo (now Tokyo) into something like a panic.*

From the outset Perry made it clear to the Japanese who were sent to confer with him that he would engage in discussions only with an official whose rank was at least the equal of his. A request of the vice-governor of Uraga that the squadron weigh anchor and withdraw to Nagasaki was firmly and indignantly spurned by Perry. Annoyed by the presence of Japanese craft which swarmed around his vessels, Perry served notice that if they did not immediately clear away he would order his ships to open fire on them. The threat was heeded.

The anticipated procrastinations of the Japanese were encountered by Perry with great tenacity and astuteness, and he steadfastly refused to talk with anyone whose rank was not sufficiently high. Finally, on July 14, 1853, two princes came to confer with him in a pavillion especially prepared for the occasion. Perry then consigned to them the President's letter to the Emperor.† When the princes again urged him to withdraw

---

* Although the Japanese had long before the arrival of Perry identified Western ships visiting Japan as " Black Ships," this term has in recent years been employed by the Japanese to specifically identify Perry's ships. (*Cf.* Eijiro Honjo, ed., *Nippon Keizai-shi Jiten*, Tokyo, Nippon Hyoron Sha, 1940, Vol. I, p. 438.)

† Perry and the officials of the United States were apparently in ignorance of the precise nature of the dual government then functioning in Japan, particularly of the exact relationship between the Shogun and the Emperor.

to Nagasaki, he stipulated that while he would depart from Japan in two or three days, he would return with an even larger squadron in the fóllowing spring, by which time he would expect the Japanese to have fully discussed the problem among themselves and be prepared to conclude a treaty. On July 17, eight days after his arrival in Edo Bay, Perry departed for China, where he planned to spend the winter.

Shortly after Perry's arrival in Edo Bay, the Russian Admiral Poutiatin had put in at Nagasaki, where he had unsuccessfully attempted to negotiate a treaty of amity and commerce for Russia. Proceeding to Shanghai, the Russian Admiral encountered Perry and suggested that they combine their efforts to secure a common treaty since the objectives of their two governments appeared to be similar. Perry tactfully rejected the proposal on the ground that alliances were not in accord with traditional American policy. Actually Perry had no desire to share with any other official the historic glory of reopening Japan to foreign intercourse, even had he had the authority to act conjointly.

While Perry was wintering in China two significant developments took place: (1) the death of the Shogun, and (2) the outbreak of the Crimean War, with Russia involved against France and Great Britain. Perry apparently feared that the Shogun's death might plunge Japan into a period of internal unrest and division. As for the Crimean War, although it was being fought in the distant Black Sea area he was manifestly concerned that its hostilities might spread to the Far East, with the belligerents possibly attempting to utilize Japan as Far Eastern bases of operation, thereby endangering the success of his mission. Perry considered his mission so urgent that despite the great Taiping Rebellion which was then raging in China, and the desirability of keeping his ships in Chinese waters to offer possibly needed succor to Americans residing in China, he was insistent on immediately returning to Japan to complete his mission.

CONSTERNATION IN JAPAN

Meanwhile, Japan was in great consternation. President Fillmore's letter, which Perry had consigned to the high officials of the Shogunate, while courteous nevertheless demanded (1) the opening of the country for commercial intercourse, (2) humane treatment for shipwrecked American sailors, and (3) the establishment of an American coaling station in Japan. These demands created a serious dilemma for the harassed Shogunate. Acceptance of them might be construed by the people as an act of subservience to a foreign power and result in serious internal uprisings. Rejection of them, on the other hand, might conceivably result in war with the United States, as Perry had not too subtly intimated. The Shogunate therefore took the unprecedented step of forwarding copies of the presidential letter to the Emperor and the highest nobles of the land and soliciting their advice on the action to be taken. The Imperial Court, which was under the influence of elements hostile to the Shogunate, insisted on continuation of the exclusion policy and rejection of all American demands regardless of the consequences. These views were shared by most of the nobles. Only a small minority of influential nobles counselled negotiating with the Americans and concluding a limited treaty to remain in effect for a short trial period.[10]

Although due consideration was given to the advice that was offered, the Shogunate after some vacillation finally decided on negotiations with Perry when he returned. In taking this decision the Shogunate acted out of selfish interest and strictly on the basis of the almost exclusive information it possessed concerning the outside world, which convinced it that a policy of resistance to the Americans would be folly and perhaps disastrous. In the meantime, however, extensive preparations were made to resist to the extent possible any American resort to the use of force. The bells of religious institutions and metal articles contributed by wealthy patriots were hastily cast into cannon. The forts guarding Edo Bay were strengthened and new fortifications were feverishly constructed. Something like 300,000 samurai warriors flocked to Edo to offer their services.

PERRY'S SECOND VISIT

On February 12, 1854 Commodore Perry arrived in Edo Bay for the second time, with twice as many warships as on the occasion of his first visit. Again he anchored at Uraga, and envoys of the Shogunate promptly informed him that plans had been completed for the conduct of the negotiations at Kamakura. Perry firmly informed the envoys that he would positively not move from his anchorage, and he warned that any further procrastination might result in most unfortunate consequences for Japan. He explicitly served notice that if necessary to complete his mission, his present formidable fleet could be quickly augmented to fifty and that as many more could be summoned from California. Fully convinced of Perry's iron determination, and also concerned lest the warring Russians, French and British might violate Japan's territorial integrity, the Shogunate consented to begin discussions at nearby Kanagawa.

The first talks were held at Kanagawa on March eighth. The Shogun's delegation consisted of an imperial plenipotentiary and four others of very high rank. Perry was given the Shogun's reply to the presidential letter, which stated that the President's demands were acceptable. On March 11 Perry delivered the presents that he had brought with him, which included firearms and swords, books, clocks, instruments and tools, a miniature railroad set, and perfumes. Twelve days later the Japanese in turn presented a number of gifts for Perry, the President and members of the party participating in the discussions.

The treaty discussions proceeded without any significant difficulties, and on March 31 the historic Treaty of Kanagawa was signed. The treaty was a very simple one, containing only a few provisions and falling far short of establishing full and adequate relations. It stipulated that there would be established between the two countries a "perfect, permanent, and universal peace and sincere and cordial amity." Trade was to be permitted on a cash and carry basis in two ports, Shimoda and Hakodate,* which might also be utilized by American ships in distress. Shipwrecked sailors were to be treated humanely, and a consulate might be established in Shimoda. In addition, the United States was to enjoy most-favored-nation privileges.

While the treaty was inadequate because of its limited coverage, and specifically because it said nothing about a coaling station, extraterritoriality or the rights of permanent residence for American citizens, it nevertheless was a historic milestone since it definitively ended the long period of Japanese seclusion and exclusion. Other Western nations shortly after concluded similar treaties. Admiral James Sterling obtained a treaty in October 1854, ratified a year later, which contained some extraterritorial privileges, provided for freedom of religion for British subjects, and opened Nagasaki and Hakodate to British ships. A Russian treaty, obtained by Admiral Poutiatin in February 1855, closely resembled the Perry treaty, and provided for the use of three ports (Nagasaki, Hakodate and Shimoda). A Dutch treaty, signed in November 1855, was largely concerned with the removal of the long-standing restrictions on Dutch trade, but it also contained some extraterritorial privileges. Since the United States enjoyed most-favored-nation privileges, its rights were therefore represented by the sum total of all these treaties.

PERRY IMMORTALIZED

The Senate promptly ratified the Treaty of Kanagawa. Shortly afterwards, the Secretary of the Navy wrote Perry as follows: "You have won additional fame for yourself, reflected new honor upon the very honorable service to which you belong, and we all hope have secured for your country, for commerce, and for

---

* Neither of these sites was very suitable for commerce.

civilization a triumph the blessings of which may be enjoyed by generations yet unborn." On his return to the United States, Perry was honored by Americans in Canton; and in the United States, New York and other cities feted him. Even European countries considered his exploit of great historic significance and accordingly lauded him.

It was the Japanese, however, who have perhaps tendered Perry the fullest recognition and honors. In February 1855, when ratifications of the Treaty of Kanagawa were exchanged in Japan, the Japanese commissioners with whom Perry had conducted the negotiations proclaimed that " his name would live forever in the history of Japan." At the turn of the century a group of Japanese organized a society for the erection of a fitting monument to the memory of Perry, whose visitation was described by them as " the most memorable event in our annals—an event which enabled the country to enter upon an unprecedented era of national ascendancy in which we are now living." Money for the monument was subscribed by all classes of Japanese society, including the Emperor. The monument was dedicated on July 14, 1901, the forty-eighth anniversary of Perry's initial landing in Japan. The inscription on the monument was written by Prince Hirobumi Ito, a leading figure in the Meiji transformation of Japan from a feudal to a relatively modern society. The president of the Perry association declared in an address that " it was at this spot that the modern civilization of our empire had its begin- ning " and the monument " is erected to preserve on stone our determina- tion never to forget the friendship of the United States that sent Commodore Perry to induce us in a peaceful way to have inter- course with foreign powers."*

---

* Manifestly the speaker, either through ignorance of the historical facts or deliberate graciousness, shut his eyes to some of the unpleasant realities of the Perry mission, doubtless to make the occasion as complete and joyful as possible.

PERRY AS PROPHET

Perry was more than a naval officer and diplomat. He possessed a penetrating insight of the dominant international forces that were then manifesting themselves. He accurately foresaw the future expansion of Russia into East Asia and her ultimate clash with vital American interests. In this realistic foresight he was far ahead of almost all the political soothsayers of his time, for in his day as for several subsequent decades it was commonly believed that the United States and Russia were bound by a considerable community of interests and that a future conflict between them had no realistic basis. In a paper which was read before the American Geographical and Statistical Society on March 6, 1856, Perry predicted:

> It requires no sage to predict events so strongly foreshadowed to us all; still " Westward " will " the course of empire take its way." But the last act of the drama is yet to be unfolded; and notwithstanding the reasoning of political empires, westward, northward and southward, to me it seems that the people of America will, in some form or other, extend their dominion and power, until they shall have brought within their mighty embrace multitudes of the islands of the great Pacific, and placed the Saxon race upon the eastern shore of Asia. And I think, too, that eastward and southward will her great rival in future aggrandizement [Russia] stretch forth her power to the coasts of China and Siam; and thus the Saxon and Cossack will meet once more, in strife or in friend-ship, on another field. Will it be friendship? I fear not! The antagonistic exponents of freedom and absolutism must meet at last, and then will be fought the mighty battle on which the world will look with breathless interest; for on its issues will depend the freedom or the slavery of the world—despotism or rational liberty must be the fate of civilized man. I think I see in the distance the giants that are growing up for that fierce and final encounter; in the progress of events that battle must sooner or later inevitably be fought.*

---

* Although Perry was referring to the despotism of the Czars, the new despotism of the Communist masters of Russia has fully matched that of the Czars in its de-gradation of human dignity and its enslavement of the mind.

CHAPTER II

THE CRITICAL TRANSITION PERIOD

While Perry's mission was a considerable diplomatic success and succeeded in opening the door that had long sealed Japan, it did not result in the peaceful overnight transition of Japan from a policy of seclusion to one of open intercourse with the outside world. The domestic enemies of the Shogunate made political capital of the concessions that had been made and for political reasons encouraged the intensification of anti-foreignism as a means of embarrassing the Shogunate and further weakening it for the final assault. Moreover, it was too much to expect that the seclusion mentality which had been assiduously cultivated over a period of two and a half centuries could be easily and smoothly transformed without incidents and without some turmoil. With the conclusion of Perry's mission and the signing of the subsequent treaties with the other powers, there consequently followed a period of more than a decade during which Japan seethed with the possibility of civil war and widespread violence against the foreigner who had in effect forced himself upon Japan.

TOWNSEND HARRIS AND THE SHIMODA CONVENTION

Fifteen days after the departure of Commodore Perry from

Edo Bay, the American clipper ship *Lady Pierce* arrived in the bay, while on a pleasure cruise, for the purpose of delivering to the Japanese authorities a shipwrecked Japanese who had been taken aboard in Honolulu. The captain of the vessel was thanked for returning the Japanese, he and his crew were courteously treated, and the vessel was furnished with supplies. The captain was informed, however, that in the future all American ships should enter the treaty port of Shimoda.[1]

In accordance with the provisions of the Treaty of Kanagawa, the United States Government in August 1855 commissioned Townsend Harris as the first American consul general to reside in Shimoda. Harris was instructed to exert all efforts toward securing full protection for Americans frequenting Shimoda, if possible to secure an audience with the Shogun, and, failing in that, to attempt to convince the Shogunate of the desirability of enlarging commercial intercourse between the United States and Japan.[2] Although his schooling was limited, Harris was well informed and had acquired a knowledge of Spanish, French and Italian. He had had some experience in public affairs, had been a merchant in New York, and had also served for six years as a super-cargo and merchant in China where he had acquired a first-hand knowledge of the Far East. Harris was a man of great tact, unusual ability, great fortitude and high moral principles. Indicative of his conscientiousness and sincerity is the entry he made in his journal as he approached the Japanese coast and he caught his first view of majestic Fujiyama: " I shall be the first recognized agent from a civilized power to reside in Japan. This forms an epoch in my life, and may be the beginning of a new order of things in Japan. I hope I may so conduct myself that I may have honorable mention in the histories which will be written on Japan and its future destiny."[3]

Harris arrived in Shimoda aboard the warship *San Jacinto* on August 21, 1856. En route he had stopped at Siam, where he negotiated a treaty with the government of that country.

As a result of his first meetings with the Japanese, Harris was

very favorably impressed by them and wrote in his journal that
" they are superior to any people east of the Cape of Good Hope."
Nevertheless, from the very outset Harris encountered obstacles
and a hostility that doubtless would have discouraged a man of
lesser fortitude and courage. The governor of Shimoda, for
example, promptly informed Harris that the arrival of a consul
had not been anticipated and that consequently no preparations
had been made to receive or accommodate one. The governor
suggested that it would be very advisable to return to the United
States. Harris indignantly refused to do so. After being warned
by Harris that if he were not properly treated in Shimoda he
would proceed at once to Edo in the *San Jacinto*, the governor
reluctantly agreed to provide a temple for living quarters. An
offer to furnish some men " to aid and protect him " was rejected by Harris, who suspected that they would be employed to
spy on him. After taking up residence in the temple, Harris
was confronted with further vexations and annoyances. Japanese
guards were stationed around the temple and even his servants
were obstructed when they went shopping for food and supplies.
By means of patience and tact, however, Harris gradually gained
the confidence of the Japanese and won their respect for his rights
as a consul.

Although commissioned as a consul general, Harris had been
vested with full diplomatic powers and the authority to engage
in treaty discussions. Shortly after his arrival he therefore informed the Shogun's minister of foreign affairs that he was prepared to begin discussions with the view of concluding a treaty
which would be more adequate than the one in effect. Discussions
for this purpose were carried on in Shimoda over a protracted
period of time, during which Harris was compelled to tolerate
the most vexatious procrastination and obstructionism. There
were times when even the persevering Harris doubted that he
could win the Japanese over to his points. Added to these difficulties, Harris was in poor health and completely isolated from
his home government, from which he did not receive a single

communication until more than a year after his arrival in Shimoda.[4]

Success finally came to Harris, however, and on June 17, 1857, ten months after his arrival in Japan, he and officials of the Shogunate affixed their signatures to the Convention of Shimoda, concluded " for the purpose of further regulating the intercourse of American citizens within the Empire of Japan." This convention clarified some of the misconceptions resulting from the Perry treaty and also embodied all that had accrued to the United States by virtue of its most-favored-nation privileges. The convention opened the port of Nagasaki for the procurement of supplies, specifically granted Americans the right of permanent residence in the treaty ports, fixed the rate of exchange for American currency at its actual value, granted extraterritorial jurisdiction to American consuls, and more clearly defined the rights and privileges of American consuls in Japan. Although Harris was ailing and somewhat discouraged when this convention was concluded, it nevertheless was a very considerable diplomatic achievement, an achievement due entirely to his own sincerity and persuasiveness without threats or material backing.[5]

In October 1857 the Dutch also concluded a new treaty with the Japanese which, inter alia, provided for a temporary import tariff of 35 percent, authorized freedom of religion for Dutch nationals within their premises, and significantly forbade the importation of opium. A Russian treaty concluded in the same month also proscribed the importation of opium. The Dutch and Russian " anti-opium " clauses rendered a singular service to Japan; it is very likely, however, that the Dutch and Russians were more motivated by a desire to strike at a key product in Britain's envied trade rather than by sincere moral convictions.[6]

THE EDO TREATY OF 1858

The Convention of Shimoda, while a noteworthy improvement on the Perry treaty, nevertheless was too limited in scope and details to meet the legitimate requirements of the United States at that time. Harris' next move, therefore, was to begin negotiations for a truly comprehensive treaty. Harris had in his possession a letter from the President of the United States, addressed to the Emperor, which he wished to deliver in person. Initially Harris was apparently ignorant of the exact nature of the so-called dual government then prevailing in Japan and of the fact that the actual ruler was the Shogun rather than the Emperor. It was not long, however, before Harris became well informed of the actual state of affairs. He then insisted on being permitted to deliver the letter personally to the Shogun's court in Edo. The Shogunate was at first strongly opposed to this desire, but finally consented for fear that Harris might employ warships to deliver the letter personally by force.

Harris made the long journey from Shimoda to Edo on horseback in November 1857, accompanied by a retinue of some 350 guards and attendants. The trip of 180 miles was made over the ancient Tokaido (the main highway) and required seven days. The Shogunate had made careful preparations for the trip of Harris and his retinue. Huge crowds assembled along the route to catch a glimpse of the " great man." No incidents of any kind took place until Harris reached the outlying districts of Edo, where the officials of the Shogun insisted on examining his baggage in accordance with provisions of the law. Harris firmly refused to permit this examination on the ground that it would be a violation of his rights as a consul. Somewhat chagrined, the officials did not press the matter and permitted Harris to continue unmolested, his baggage untouched. Harris arrived in Edo on a Sunday, and hundreds of thousands of curious Japanese observed the pompous entrance in silence. A devout Protestant, Harris refused to conduct any business on that day since it was the Sabbath. " Ever since I have been in this country," he wrote in his journal, " I have refused to transact any business on that day." The Japanese apparently understood his motive and respected him for it.

Harris' arrival in Edo was of historic significance, since it marked the first time since 1613* that a foreign representative had been received in audience by the Shogun. After calling on the principal ministers of state, Harris was presented to the Shogun,† to whom he personally delivered the President's letter. After the audience, in which the Japanese were considerably impressed by his dignified bearing, Harris retired to his apartment and there was the recipient of a special elaborate dinner sent by the Shogun. The usual presents were then exchanged, and thereafter Harris set to work in earnest to discuss the comprehensive treaty required by his government.

Although the Japanese had ceased to be hostile and by this time had actually come to have a very high regard for Harris, his task was not easy, primarily because of the almost total ignorance of the Japanese concerning the nature of diplomatic relations on a basis of equality. Aware of this ignorance to which they frankly confessed and for which they begged enlightenment, Harris obligingly and painstakingly explained many things to them, such as the rank of a minister, his duties, the fundamental principles of international law, and the characteristics of Western governments and economic systems. The following entry in his journal is particularly interesting and refreshing: " I may be said to be engaged in teaching the elements of political economy to the Japanese. They said they were in the dark on these points, and were like children ; therefore I must have patience with them."

By means of patience, sympathetic understanding, tact and sharp acumen, Harris finally succeeded in overcoming the hesitation of the Japanese. His candidness and sincerity gained the complete confidence of the Japanese officials, and he further ingratiated himself with them by yielding on a number of minor points which

---

* In that year the British envoy Captain Saris had been received in audience by the Shogun.

† Prior to the audience Harris had obtained the consent of the Shogun's officials for the substitution of three bows, as was customary in European receptions, for the traditional kowtow expected of all when presented to the Shogun.

he knew they could concede only with the greatest difficulties, if at all.   Harris clinched his objective, however, by skilfully playing on the fears of the Japanese concerning the intentions of the avidly imperialistic powers, such as Great Britain, France and Russia.   He warned Lord Hotta, the Shogun's enlightened prime minister, that as soon as the British and the French concluded the war they were then waging with China (the Arrow War) they would dispatch fleets to Japan to demand important concessions. He suggested that Japan could best protect herself by establishing full treaty relations with the Western powers, who would consequently serve as a check on the aggressive intentions of each other in Japan.   The United States, he reassuringly and correctly pointed out, did not permit the acquisition of territory overseas. Moreover, he said, there was no danger whatsoever of the United States and Japan becoming enemies, regardless of whether or not the desired treaty was concluded.   He cautioned, however, that if Japan failed to establish satisfactory treaty relations with the Western powers, she might become the victim of grave misfortunes, caused not by the United States but by the other less scrupulous Western powers.   "If you accept the treaty I now offer you, no other country will demand more," he explained to Lord Hotta. "If I display the treaty to the Europeans, they will desire to conclude identical treaties, and the matter will be settled by the mere sending over of a minister."

The Imperial Court in Kyoto, which, as indicated, was strongly influenced by powerful western daimyos now openly hostile to the Tokugawa Shogunate, was opposed to the treaty and refused to sanction it.   Seemingly an impasse had been reached, since the Shogun, conscious of his waning power, dared not oppose what purported and appeared to be the imperial will backed by the people.   On the other hand, the Shogun and his officials were fully aware of the grave danger threatening Japan and of the absolute necessity of establishing satisfactory relations as a means of discouraging acts of aggression on the part of the foreign powers, as Harris had explained.

The hesitation of the Shogunate came to an end when Lord Naosuke Ii was appointed Tairo, or Senior Minister, of the Shogunate. A man of strong character, determination and political acumen, Naosuke Ii believed that failure to conclude the treaty would be blind folly and a needless invitation to disaster. Accordingly, he assumed full responsibility and ordered the Harris treaty to be signed, regardless of the refusal of the Imperial Court to sanction it. For this bold action, he incurred the intense hatred of the pro-imperialists and the anti-foreigners. He was subsequently assassinated, in 1860, but later generations of Japanese came to regard him as one of the great men of modern Japan who had the courage to render the nation a singular service in a critical hour.

The Harris treaty was at length signed in Edo Bay aboard the U.S.S. *Powhattan*, on July 29, 1858. It was the first real treaty of commerce concluded by Japan since the beginning of the seventeenth century, and served as a model for treaties subsequently negotiated by the other powers. It provided for the opening of three ports to trade and two others to visitation and residence,* the establishment of an American ministry in Edo, and extraterritorial jurisdiction for American diplomatic and consular representatives in Japan. The extraterritorial provisions had in fact been reluctantly insisted upon by Harris, and he subsequently stated that their inclusion was against his conscience and that he hoped they would some day be abolished. The treaty also invited the Japanese to study naval construction in the United States, and a unique clause, at that time typical of American diplomacy in Asia, provided for the mediation of the President of the United

---

* Kanagawa, Niigata and Hyogo (Kobe) were opened to commerce, and Edo (Tokyo) and Osaka were opened to visitation and residence. Shimoda, because of its inadequacy as a commercial port, was to be closed. After the new treaties went into effect Lord Naosuke Ii created a new port at Yokohama for the purpose of removing foreigners from Kanagawa, through which passed the famous Tokaido. He feared that unless the foreigners were removed from Kanagawa serious incidents might arise, since the proud and bold samurai used the Tokaido extensively.

States between Japan and other powers should the occasion arise and should it be requested. Either government could request the revision of the treaty after July 4, 1871. The commercial regulations which supplemented the treaty provided for a sliding scale of duties on imports and a flat five percent duty on all exports. The duties could be revised in 1864 on the request of the Japanese Government.

Without the support of warships or armaments of any kind and without invoking threats, either open or veiled, Harris had succeeded through tact and brilliant diplomacy alone in achieving one of the most outstanding successes in the history of the foreign service of the State Department. Whereas Perry was the first to break the hard shell of Tokugawa seclusion-exclusion, Harris paved the way for the establishment of full commercial relations with the nations of the West on a basis of reasonableness and dignity. In a sense, too, Harris prepared the way for the eventual admission of Japan as an equal member in the comity of nations.

Treaties similar to the one negotiated by Harris were immediately concluded by Great Britain, France, Russia and the Netherlands. The British treaty was negotiated by the illustrious Lord Elgin, who called on Harris at Shimoda to secure a copy of his treaty for use as a model and also to employ on a temporary basis his secretary, Henry Heusken, as an interpreter. The British treaty, however, provided for the reduction of import tariffs on cotton and woolen manufactured goods from twenty to five percent. It is to be noted that this provision, when implemented, caused great injury to the native textile industry and greatly handicapped its modernization, since Japanese producers could not compete with the low cost of the industrially produced British products. All the treaties concluded by the Shogunate were approved by imperial edict on February 2, 1859 as temporary measures to keep foreigners at a safe distance and to serve merely as a prelude to the ultimate restoration of the ruptured seclusion policy.[8]

The Harris treaty provided for the exchange of ratifications in Washington. To accomplish this purpose a Japanese mission consisting of 71 persons sailed from Japan in February 1860 aboard the American warship *Powhattan*. The mission was warmly welcomed in San Francisco and Washington. The courteous conduct and native intelligence of the Japanese greatly impressed the Americans. The American press noted that " they were quite as dignified, intelligent, and well bred as any gentlemen in any country or time."[9]

Following the ratification of the American treaty, Harris was commissioned as Minister to Japan, a post he held until 1862 when he was relieved at his own request. He gave as his reasons for resigning the following: " The extraordinary life of isolation I have been compelled to lead has greatly impaired my health, and this, joined to my advancing years, warns me that it is time for me to give up all public employment." Just as they had commemorated Commodore Perry with the erection of an appropriate monument, so did later generations of Japanese remember Townsend Harris with the erection of a monument in Tokyo, which was unveiled on December 18, 1936.

A PERIOD OF INTENSE ANTI-FOREIGNISM

The attempt of the Shogunate to enforce the treaties of 1858 and open the country to widened foreign intercourse accentuated the discontent that had been smoldering for some time against the Tokugawa Government. Part of the accentuated discontent was directed against the rapidly weakening Shogunate, and part was directed against the foreigner. Forces hostile to the Shogunate, particularly the Imperial Court in Kyoto and the rebellious clans of the west, capitalized on the unpopularity of the treaties and the apparent responsibility of the Shogunate for their conclusion. Indeed, during this critical period anti-Tokugawaism and anti-foreignism were almost synonymous terms. " Revere the Emperor and expel the barbarians " became a popular catchphrase epitomizing the explosive unrest of the time.

The period of intense anti-foreignism lasted from the date of the conclusion of the treaties of 1858 to about 1865 when the Emperor sanctioned the treaties. From then until 1868 the fury of anti-foreignism abated considerably. After the overthrow of the Tokugawa Government in 1868, the Imperial Government switched from its former apparent support of anti-foreignism to a policy of assiduously favoring increased foreign intercourse. With this change in imperial policy, however, anti-foreignism did not immediately die down completely. Actually it remained as a force of considerable importance, although a minor and diminishing one, until about 1894.

During the period of intense anti-foreignism the Shogunate apparently acted in good faith and attempted to do all it could to comply with the provisions of the treaties. Harris understood the dilemma and difficulties of the Shogunate, and refused to hold it responsible for the lawless acts of individuals over whom it actually had little if any control under the circumstances of the times. This, of course, was only one of the manifestations of the moral greatness of Harris, especially when one considers that his life had actually been threatened when he was negotiating the treaty. The other foreign representatives, however, did not possess Harris' sympathy and understanding, and in general they favored a tough policy. Secretary of State Seward also advocated a tough policy, and he believed there was a real danger the foreigners might actually be expelled from some or all of the treaty ports. He informed Harris that " very large interests, not of our own country, but of the civilized world, are involved in retaining the foothold of foreign nations already acquired in the Empire of Japan."[10] Happily for all concerned, Harris adroitly softened the toughness advocated by his superior, the Secretary of State.

The first serious anti-foreign outbreak occurred in 1859 on the occasion of the visit of a Russian fleet to Yokohama when one officer and two sailors were attacked in the streets. The officer and one of the sailors were killed. In the following year the interpreter of the Russian legation was mortally wounded and the captains of two Dutch vessels were hacked to pieces. It was in March of that year that Naosuke Ii was assassinated by a band of ronin, or " masterless samurai," allegedly for " making foreign intercourse his chief aim."

In January 1861 Henry Heusken, Harris' interpreter, was murdered in the streets of Edo. On learning of this outrage, Secretary Seward suggested a joint naval demonstration by the United States, France, Great Britain and Russia to compel Japan to honor the stipulations of the treaties. Harris wisely disapproved of the suggestion, and Seward reluctantly abandoned it. Nevertheless, on December 13, 1862 Seward instructed Harris to advise Japan that she " can only have friendship or even peace with the United States by protecting the citizens and subjects of foreign powers from domestic violence." It is difficult to determine precisely how much of this " toughness " in Seward should be attributed to the exigencies of the American Civil War then raging and his compelling desire to remain on the friendliest terms possible with the great European powers, whose governments were generally sympathetic to the South.[11]

In 1862 the British legation was attacked and two of its Japanese guards were killed. In that same year the arrogant Englishman, Charles Richardson, was assaulted and murdered by some retainers of the Daimyo of Satsuma. The British Government held the Shogunate responsible for this act and demanded and obtained from it an indemnity of $500,000. In addition, the British bombarded Kagoshima, the capital of the recalcitrant daimyo, and forced him to pay an additional indemnity of $125,000. The anti-foreign elements had been greatly inflamed and emboldened by the seizure of the island of Tsushima in the previous year by a Russian admiral. The Russian defied the Shogunate and withdrew only after the British minister had intervened on the request of the Shogunate. Harris particularly regretted this incident.[12]

As an immediate result of the Richardson murder, the foreign diplomatic representatives stationed in Edo withdrew to Yokohama, where they could be protected by the guns of the foreign warships at anchor in the harbor. Harris however refused to leave Edo. In his attitude toward the anti-foreign outbreaks Harris differed sharply with the other foreign diplomats. He insisted that the harassed Shogunate was doing everything it could to honor its treaty responsibilities while the foreign diplomats, on their part, were expecting too much and the impossible under the circumstances then prevailing. He strongly maintained that none of the foreign powers should exploit the chaotic situation and the compromised position of the Shogunate to press unreasonable demands or resort to actions that would further compromise or weaken the Shogunate. In a note to Sir Rutherford Alcock, the British minister, he lamented: " I had hoped that the page of future history might record the great fact that in one spot in the Eastern world the advent of Christian civilization did not bring with it its usual attendants of rapine and bloodshed; this fond hope, I fear, is to be disappointed. I would sooner see all the treaties with this country torn up, and Japan return to its old state of isolation, than witness the horrors of war inflicted on this peaceful and happy land."[13]

The British bombardment of Kagoshima failed to intimidate the Japanese or put an end to the anti-foreign outbreaks. In 1863 the American legation in Edo was mysteriously burned. The captain of the U.S.S. *Wyoming*, then in Japanese waters, was instructed to use all the force necessary to protect American lives.[14] Robert Pruyn, who had replaced Harris, then reluctantly left Edo and joined his colleagues in Yokohama, where British and French troops had just been landed. A conscientious and able diplomat, Pruyn like Harris took a position of sympathetic understanding regarding the Shogunate and its vexatious problems. He nevertheless exerted all his efforts to protect American rights. By negotiation he was able to obtain from the Shogunate an indemnity of $10,000 for the burning of the legation and an additional $10,000 as indemnification for the Dutch mother of the murdered Heusken.

CLIMAX AND RECESSION OF ANTI-FOREIGNISM

Meanwhile, in compliance with a demand of the Emperor, the Shogun made a personal appearance at the Imperial Court in Kyoto. This action was a further indication of the rapidly deteriorating position of the Shogunate, for it marked the first time since 1634 that a Shogun had made an appearance at the court in Kyoto.[15] The Shogun departed for Kyoto in March 1863. Shortly after his arrival in Kyoto, a council of nobles decided that July 25, 1863 would be established as the day for beginning action to close the country and expel the foreigners. In Kyoto the Shogun was detained for nearly three months against his will, but he finally managed to get away and returned to Edo late in July.[16] On July 25, the appointed day for beginning the expulsion of foreigners, officials of the Shogunate in compliance with the alleged imperial will informed the foreign diplomatic representatives that imperial instructions had been received for closing the ports and expelling the foreigners. The Shogun, immediately after his return to Edo, conscientiously dispatched a memorial to the Emperor in which he advised that the time was inopportune for any attempt at the expulsion of the foreigners. The more enlightened members of the Imperial Court shared these views, but the chauvinistic elements were only further provoked. At any rate, the Shogun hesitated to enforce the order.

When informed by the Shogun's officials of the expulsion order, the foreign diplomats warned that their governments were prepared to engage in whatever military protection might be necessary.[17] On this issue, Pruyn sided with his diplomatic colleagues, and he cautioned the Shogunate that the closing of the ports would mean war with the United States as well as with the other powers. In so informing the Shogunate, Pruyn was carrying out the specific instructions of Secretary Seward to the effect " You will represent to the minister of foreign affairs that it is not at all to be expected that any of the maritime powers will consent to the suspension of their treaties, and that the United States will cooperate with them in all necessary means to maintain and secure the fulfillment of the treaties on the part of the Japanese government." In taking this firm position of collaboration with foreign powers, Seward was unquestionably primarily motivated by the exigency which required the friendliest relations possible with Great Britain and France, the nations with important interests in Japan, which were then being most ardently courted by the Confederacy.

One of the most serious anti-foreign outbreaks occurred in June and July 1863 when the Daimyo of Choshu, in giving concrete support to the Emperor's alleged desire to suspend foreign intercourse, closed the straits of Shimonoseki to foreign traffic and fired on American, French and Dutch ships in the area. The American warship *Wyoming* happened to be in Yokohama at the time and its captain obtained the approval of Minister Pruyn to engage in a retaliatory action. Proceeding to the Shimonoseki area, the *Wyoming* sank an armed steamer and a brig belonging to the Daimyo of Choshu, at a cost of four killed and seven wounded. Pruyn incidentally believed that this action strengthened the hands of the Shogunate and that it moreover served to discourage other anti-foreign daimyos from engaging in similar acts of provocation. The haughty daimyo remained unchastened until September 1863, however, when an allied expedition of British, French, Dutch and American warships heavily bombarded Shimonoseki.* With one of its most inveterate and influential enemies thus humbled, the Shogunate drew fresh courage and informed the foreign diplomats that temporizing was no longer necessary and that the treaties would be fully respected. The Shogunate of its own volition assumed full responsibility for the Choshu incident, and in October 1864 concluded a convention with the injured nations which provided for the payment of an indemnity of $3,000,000, of which $750,000 was to accrue to the United States.

---

* The allied expedition consisted of one American, three French, four Dutch and nine British vessels.

In November 1865 the Shogunate happily informed the foreign diplomats that the Emperor had at last fully sanctioned the treaties of 1858 and that the tariffs would be revised downward as desired by their governments. This development was of great significance, for it weakened the anti-foreign elements and also to a considerable extent lessened the dependence of the foreign diplomats on the Shogunate.

The Shimonoseki indemnity remained unappropriated in the United States Treasury until 1883 when the Congress, its conscience awakened, voted to return it to Japan. By this time the Shogunate had been overthrown and the Emperor had been restored to nominal power. The Imperial Government expressed its profound gratitude and expressed the hope that this instance of traditional American generosity would " tend to strengthen the mutual confidence and the feeling of good-will and friendship which at present happily subsists between the peoples of our respective countries."

CHAPTER III

A LONG PERIOD OF CORDIAL
RELATIONS

THE IMPERIAL RESTORATION

In 1868 the Shogunate was overthrown in a relatively bloodless revolution and the boy emperor, Mutsuhito, was ostensibly restored as the real ruler of Japan.* Actually the governing power was merely transferred from the Tokugawas to the leading clansmen of the west and the imperial nobility. The Emperor remained essentially a figurehead, and his power was fundamentally restricted to the theory that the new Government administered for him and in accordance with his wishes. Be that as it may, the new Government demonstrated a remarkable vitality, ability and open-mindedness in dealing with the vastly changed situation in which Japan found herself. Gone was most of the blind conservatism and xenophobia which had seemingly once animated many of the elements now included in the Government. The new Government promptly and intelligently applied itself to the task of modernizing Japan so that she might take her place among the great nations of the world and be able to defend herself and vigorously promote her national interests. Much of the old feudal system was swept away, something resembling a modern

---

* Mutsuhito is generally known in history by his reign name, Meiji. In September 1868 Edo was renamed Tokyo, or Eastern Capital, and in March 1869 it became the actual capital and residence of the Emperor.

representative government was established, universal education was adopted, and an impressive beginning was made in the direction of industrialization. In the great task of modernization, advice and technicians were wisely solicited throughout the world. By the end of the century, in a period of only a few decades, Japan stood forth as the strongest and most modern country in Asia, with an army and navy capable of compelling respect from any would-be aggressor.

In the field of foreign relations, the new Government promptly adopted a policy of friendlier and widened relations with the outside world. Anti-foreignism remained a factor, but discouraged by the Government it progressively declined in significance.

UNPOPULARITY OF THE UNILATERAL TREATIES

A new Tariff Convention had been negotiated and signed on June 25, 1866 between officials of the Shogunate and representatives of the United States, Great Britain, France and the Netherlands. However, the convention was not submitted to either the Shogun or the Emperor, and the Shogun's officials are alleged to have made it clear that it would remain in force temporarily and only for a few years. Actually it remained in force until August 1899.[1]

The Tariff Convention was unilateral in its benefits; that is to say, in favor of the foreign powers and at the expense of Japan. It provided for an ad valorem duty of five percent on a specified list of articles and lower specific duties on 89 articles based on their average price during the preceding five years. Goods that could be admitted duty free were specified and the importation of opium was prohibited.[2] The convention was subject to revision after July 1, 1871, provided that both contracting parties were agreeable.

After the Restoration of 1868 the principal Japanese objective in foreign policy was to obtain a revision of the unilateral treaties which were offensive to the national pride and injurious to the national interest. The unilateral treaties were particularly odious because they deprived Japan of two very important sovereign rights: (1) the right to regulate her own tariffs and thereby protect her commercial and industrial interests, and (2) the right to subject aliens to the law and judicial system of the land. It was rightfully felt by the Japanese that as long as these humiliating restrictions remained in force, Japan could not hope to be admitted as an equal member in the comity of nations.

By this time most of the foreign powers were not uncompromisingly opposed to revision. However, whereas the Japanese wanted revision as a sovereign right, the foreign powers, with the exception of the United States, insisted on revisions on a quid pro quo basis. Despite these divergent views, the Japanese Government on several occasions between 1869 and 1871 sounded out the foreign diplomats in Tokyo. The overtures were in general coldly received, and it became very apparent to the Japanese that revision was a major problem and likely to require a long time for its consummation. The Terashima Memorandum, presented to the foreign diplomats in Tokyo in 1871, is indicative of what the Japanese Government was willing to accept for the time being; among other things, it asked for reciprocity, standardization of all treaty texts, and reservation of the coastal trade to Japanese nationals.[3]

Late in 1871 a Japanese mission headed by Prince Tomomi Iwakura, comprising more than a hundred officials and servants,* departed for the United States and Europe with the object of studying Western institutions and making soundings on the problem of treaty revisions. In the United States the mission found President Grant and Secretary of State Hamilton Fish sympathetic to the idea of wholesale treaty revision, but in Europe almost no encouragement was received. In fact, Great Britain was pronouncedly hostile to the idea of revision, and until 1890 was the

---

* Among the members of this mission were Takayoshi Kido, Toshimichi Okubo, Hirobumi Ito and Naoyoshi Yamaguchi, men who later distinguished themselves as leaders of the new and powerful Japan that was emerging.

leading nation opposing it. The mission returned to Japan in September 1873, nearly two years after its departure, wiser for all that it had seen and studied but having failed to achieve anything concrete in the direction of treaty revision.

Since the backwardness of Japan's laws and judicial system was the principal argument advanced by the treaty powers for refusing to surrender extraterritoriality, the Japanese now concentrated on reforming their legal codes and revising the judicial system in conformity with those prevailing in the more advanced countries of Europe. Some distinguished European jurists were employed as advisers for this purpose, among them being the great French jurist Gustave Boissonade. By 1882 the Japanese had succeeded in bringing about substantial reforms in their legal system and they believed that it now compared favorably with those of the West.

The Japanese then contended that no foreign power could any longer conscientiously argue that the legal system of Japan was barbarous and that it hence precluded the surrender of extraterritoriality. The Western powers, however, still considered the Japanese judicial system unacceptable and refused to surrender extraterritoriality, although they did express a willingness to make some concessions. Concerning the obstinacy of the Western powers in this respect, ex-President Grant in 1879 commented that " It seems incredible that rights which Western nations all regard as sacred and inviolable, because absolutely essential to their independence and dignity, should be denied by them to China and Japan."[4]

Public opinion in Japan was extremely hostile to any concessions on the extraterritorial issue and apparently demanded nothing less than the total abolition of extraterritoriality. So strong was popular feeling on this issue that no Japanese official dared to defy it. The abuses of extraterritoriality on the part of the Western nations further aggravated the problem. As in China, foreign offenders were generally acquitted or let off leniently by the consuls who tried them. It is to be noted, however, that American officials in Japan probably exercised the right of extraterritoriality more conscientiously than did any others.

Between 1873 and 1885 the American diplomatic representative in Japan was John A. Bingham, a man of considerable experience in public affairs, able and of high ideals. He advocated the restoration of full tariff autonomy to Japan and the abolition of extraterritoriality as soon as an acceptable judicial system was established in Japan. Before the termination of his tour of duty in Japan, he took the position that the Japanese had in fact established such a judicial system and that the continuation of extraterritoriality was accordingly a rank injustice. During his tour of duty he persistently opposed any interpretation of the treaties which might serve further to weaken the sovereignty of Japan, and he strongly held that even though extraterritoriality remained in force the foreigners should fully abide by the laws of Japan.[5]

PROGRESS TOWARD TREATY REVISION

Meanwhile, however, some progress was being made in the direction of treaty revision. In 1878 the United States and Japan had concluded a convention which annulled the then existing tariffs and enabled Japan to establish her own tariff schedules. Since American commercial interests linked with Japan would be ruined if the provisions of this treaty were not applicable to all nations, it was stipulated that the convention would not come into force until the other powers had concluded similar treaties. In 1882, Count Inoue, the Japanese Foreign Minister, held a conference with the foreign diplomats in Tokyo in which tariff revision and the abolition of extraterritoriality were discussed. No positive results came out of the conference because of the recalcitrance of all the foreign representatives except Bingham. In 1886 the American Minister, Richard B. Hubbard, concluded an Extradition Convention of great significance to Japan. In the words of President Cleveland, this convention was concluded not merely to facilitate criminal procedure " but also because of the support which its conclusion would give Japan in her efforts towards judicial autonomy and complete sovereignty." Great Britain refused to conclude a similar convention, and insisted that her extraterritorial privileges required Japan to extradite any British subjects who might be wanted for violations of British law.

Mexico was the first Western nation to conclude a treaty, in February 1887, which recognized the full fiscal and judicial autonomy of Japan. This treaty included a conventional most-favored-nation clause for the purpose of precluding other nations from enjoying its benefits without having made similar concessions. Drafts of new treaties were then drawn up with the United States, Germany and Russia which contained compromises, particularly regarding extraterritoriality, but public indignation, based on hostility to any compromising on the extraterritorial issue, was so great that the Japanese Foreign Minister, Count Okuma, was forced to withdraw them. Further progress was made by the Japanese, however, when the Portuguese Government in 1892 withdrew its consular representatives from Japan as an economy measure. The Japanese promptly exploited this development to assert Japanese jurisdiction over Portuguese subjects remaining in Japan, and an imperial ordinance of July 1892 denounced the treaty provisions with Portugal concerning consular jurisdiction over Portuguese nationals. These actions elicited no protest from the Portuguese Government.

Important as were these gains, the Japanese were primarily concerned with revising the treaties in force with the great powers. Only when these powers had made the necessary treaty revisions could Japan enjoy that full diplomatic equality which was then the major objective in foreign policy. Accordingly the Japanese turned to the nation with the largest interests in Japan, namely Great Britain, believing that if she could be brought to terms the other great powers would promptly fall in line.* Preliminary

---

* Ironically, Great Britain was the nation that had most persistently opposed treaty revision.

negotiations were begun in 1893 but without much success. By this time, however, the British were prepared to abandon their persistent anti-revision policy and even to go much further and lay the groundwork for an entente with Japan. The reason for this change of attitude was purely political; the intense imperialistic rivalry with Russia, as well as with Germany and France, made it desirable for Britain to cultivate Japan as a potential ally in the event of far-flung hostilities. The " splendid isolation " that for so long had served Britain so well was no longer adequate in a world bristling with armaments and seething with Anglophobia.

In 1894 negotiations proceeded slowly but smoothly, and on July 16 a new Anglo-Japanese Treaty of Commerce and Navigation was signed. Its major provisions stipulated that: (1) consular jurisdiction, or extraterritoriality, was to be completely abolished by 1899; (2) certain specified articles were to remain subject to a conventional tariff of five to ten percent ad valorem, but Japan was to regulate the import duties on all other articles beginning in 1899; (3) all of Japan was to be opened to the residence of British subjects, although they were not to be granted the right to own land.

In February 1894 the United States, which had been highly in favor of Japan's treaty negotiations with the British, began discussions with the view of concluding a similar treaty. Such a treaty was negotiated and signed on November 22. It was promptly ratified by the Senate. Unlike the British treaty, however, it demanded no tariff concessions of any kind and accordingly conceded complete tariff autonomy to the Japanese. Because of its most-favored-nation clause, however, the United States enjoyed the tariff advantages of the British treaty. By February 1898 Japan had revised her treaties with fifteen other nations, and by June 1899 treaty revisions had been made with an additional four nations. The treaties concluded between 1894 and 1899 technically gave Japan " near-equality; " but not until 1911, when tariffs were placed on a quid pro quo basis, did

Japan actually attain full equality.

The foreigners residing in Japan had been apprehensive of treaty revisions, and feared that with the abandonment of extra-territoriality they would be subjected to legal inequities and a train of abuses and injustices. These fears proved to be totally un-founded, and subsequent years demonstrated that foreigners and their property rights were as secure and as fairly treated in Japan as in any advanced Western country.

EARLY JAPANESE EXPANSIONISM AND AMERICA[6]

During the early years of the Meiji period Japan was confronted with an aggressive Western imperialism which had already severely mauled China, obliterated many so-called backward countries, and was in effect a threat to the territorial integrity of the Japanese Empire. The most feared of these imperialist nations was Russia, which in 1860 had resumed its Far Eastern expansion and sub-sequently laid claim to all of Sakhalin and the Kurile Islands, to which the Japanese had sounder historical claims than the Rus-sians. Some responsible elements in Japan for a time seriously feared the possibility of an agreement among Russia, France and Great Britain for the partitioning of Japan. In view of this threatening imperialism, it was therefore but natural that the Japanese should consider the defense of the Empire a cardinal objective of the national policy. From the determination to provide adequate defense there consequently arose the urge to obtain advance outposts to keep the imperialistic nations at as great a distance as possible.

On the other hand, there were historic forces within Japan which encouraged territorial aggrandizement per se as a symbol of imperial greatness. Expansionism and aggrandizement of the Empire had been urged by imperial supporters even before the Imperial Restoration, and a Choshu patriot had opined that the restoration of the Emperor to his powers would result in the acquisition of an extensive domain that would include Formosa, the Kurile Islands, Sakhalin, Kamchatka, Korea and a large part of Manchuria and Siberia.[7]   In March 1858 when Lord Hotta was arguing for imperial ratification of the Harris Convention, he offered the argument that after Japan became a member of the family of nations " Our national prestige and position thus insured, the nations of the world will come to look up to our Emperor as the Great Ruler of all nations, and they will come to follow our policy and submit themselves to our judgement."[8] This expansionist heritage, while moderate, was fanned by the imperialism of the West which the Japanese eagerly adopted as a concomitant of a great and virile power.

The urge for expansionism was further stimulated by the industrial revolution which was having its beginnings in Japan. Whereas agrarian Tokugawa Japan had been practically self-sufficient, the new Japan that was rapidly becoming industrialized required increasing sources of raw materials and expanded markets for the products of its factories.   As Japan became more industrialized, this economic impetus to imperialism became increasingly more intensified.

Defense and expansionism require an adequate military force. Such a force was lacking in Japan when the Imperial Restoration took place, but it was quickly established as a result of the government purchase of war equipment, the government support of incipient war industries, and the employment of foreign military advisers.   During the early part of the Meiji period, the need for a strong military establishment was dictated largely by defensive and security considerations, but toward the close of the century armed power became the tool of expansionism.

Up to the beginning of the twentieth century, the territorial aspirations of the Japanese were extremely modest in comparison with those of the great imperialistic powers of the West.   Since this was an age when imperialism held a respected status among the so-called highly civilized nations, and considering also that the United States had done considerable expanding on its own account and that many American expansionists were casting covetous eyes at the Caribbean area, almost no one in the United States appeared to be in the least disturbed by what saber rattling there was in Japan. This American forbearance was perhaps most influenced by the fact that Japanese actions and known intentions did not threaten any real American interests in the slightest degree.

By the end of the nineteenth century the new Japan had dispatched a punitive expedition to the lawless island of Formosa, had definitively annexed the Ryukyu and Bonin islands, had acquired acknowledged control over the Kurile Islands and the southern half of Sakhalin, and had engaged in a major war with China. The details of these developments are, of course, beyond the scope of this volume. Here only the role of the United States need be noted.

In 1861, as has been indicated, a Russian naval commander occupied the island of Tsushima for a potential naval base and had barracks constructed there for a small military force. Several protests were made by the Shogunate, but it was powerless at that time to add the weight of military force to its arguments. Being fully aware of the intense rivalry between Great Britain and Russia, the Shogunate consequently turned to Britain for support. Secretary Seward offered to serve as mediator, and he somewhat naively informed Minister Harris that " I will, in the name of this government, as the friend of Japan, as well as of Russia, seek from the latter explanations which I should hope would be satisfactory to Japan."[9] Nothing came of this offer, but as a result of strong British remonstration, including the dispatch of Admiral Sir James Hope with two warships, the Russians finally vacated the island peacefully.

Late in 1861 the Shogunate informed Minister Harris that Japan intended to " reoccupy " the Bonin Islands and pledged that the rights of Americans there would be respected. Commander John Kelly had formally taken possession of these islands in 1853 on instructions from his superior, Commodore Perry, but the State Department had never sanctioned the seizure. In

1873 Secretary Fish formally renounced all claims to any part of the islands. Great Britain also surrendered its claims to these islands, and hence they were left to the exclusive possession of Japan.[10]

Beginning about 1876 Japan and China became engaged in a bitter rivalry over the status of the Korean Kingdom and the control of its affairs. This rivalry erupted into a formal war in August 1894, fought chiefly on Korean soil, which terminated in the following year with a decisive Japanese victory. Prior to the formal outbreak of this war, the great European powers were contemplating some form of intervention against Japan. The United States, however, refused to become a party to any multi-power action directed against Japan. Efforts of the decrepit Korean Government in June to enlist American support against Japan also failed. On June 9 Secretary Gresham made it clear to the Korean Minister in Washington that the United States intended to view the Korean question with " impartial neutrality " and that it would deal with Japan only in a " friendly way."[11] At the same time, Gresham conscientiously informed the Japanese Minister that he hoped Japan would deal " kindly and fairly with her feeble neighbor."[12]

Throughout the period of hostilities between China and Japan, the United States continued to maintain an effective neutrality and impartiality toward both belligerents and firmly refused to become associated with any European machinations intended to harm either China or Japan. Categorically rejected was a proposal by the British Minister, of October 8, that the United States, Russia, Germany, France and Great Britain intervene jointly to terminate the war on the basis of an indemnity to be paid by China and a multi-power guarantee of Korea's independence.

With the war going badly against her, China in November appealed to President Cleveland for the good offices of the United States. Cleveland replied that the United States would mediate only if both belligerents requested its good offices. Meanwhile,

Secretary Gresham instructed the American Minister in Tokyo to inquire if the Japanese Government desired American mediation. Gresham's instructions pointed out that while " Our attitude toward both belligerents is that of an impartial and friendly neutral, desiring the welfare of both," it nevertheless was not unlikely that the great powers might intervene and force a settlement that would be disadvantageous to Japan. Gresham clearly saw through the guise of the European powers ; he knew that they were not concerned about the welfare of either Korea or China, but rather that they wanted Japan expelled from all influence on the continent so that the partitioning of China might be resumed.[13]   Japan however courteously rejected the American offer of mediation, and made it clear to China that peace could be obtained only by direct negotiations between China and Japan.*   Beaten on the field of battle and unable to count on the friendly intervention of the great powers, China finally agreed to direct negotiations, which terminated in the Treaty of Shimonoseki.

Indicative of the esteem in which both China and Japan held the United States throughout the war were their requests for American diplomats to handle the interests of their nationals in the respective enemy countries for the duration of hostilities. After the conclusion of peace the Emperor of Japan personally wrote to President Cleveland thanking him for his humanitarian attitude during the war and the efforts of American diplomatic representatives in Tokyo and Peking to bring the Chinese and Japanese together for peace discussions. The actions of the United States during the war, he noted, " served to draw still closer the bonds of friendship and good brotherhood which happily unite our two countries."[14]

---

* Great Britain, while initially not friendly to Japan, later shifted to a policy of benevolent neutrality toward Japan. (Dennett, op. cit., p. 158–160.)

HAWAII, THE PHILIPPINES AND JAPAN

In 1894 Americans and Europeans residing in Hawaii fomented a revolution which resulted in the overthrow of the native monarch and the establishment of a provisional republic. Later that year the leaders of the provisional republic concluded a treaty of annexation with the United States. On learning of the treaty of annexation, the Japanese Government, concerned for the welfare of the large number of Japanese who had emigrated there, formally informed the United States that the continuation of cordial relations depended on the maintenance of an independent Hawaii. Japan withdrew its protest, however, when assured by the American Government that in the event of annexation the rights of Japanese nationals would be fully protected. With this assurance, which was faithfully carried out, the Japanese Government manifested a friendly attitude toward the inevitable annexation, which was carried out in 1898.

Little need here be said of the American war with Spain in 1898 and the American acquisition of the Philippine Islands. While some Japanese regarded the advent of America into the far Pacific with some misgivings, the Japanese Government maintained a very correct position and expressed no objections to the American retention of the islands.

THE " MODEL " PERIOD OF RELATIONS IN RETROSPECT

In recapitulating it is to be noted that with minor and infrequent exceptions the period from 1868 to the end of the century was one of official and unofficial American friendliness for Japan. The United States to a considerable degree regarded emergent Japan as something like a Pacific ward for whose welfare it had a moral responsibility. The United States asked for no special privileges and it was consistently willing to surrender the unilateral rights it possessed if the other powers would do likewise. The sympathetic understanding of the great American diplomatic representatives in Tokyo, like Harris, Pruyn and Bingham, has been quite properly emphasized in this discussion.   Unofficially, too, many Americans contributed their talents to the modernization of Japan, particularly in the field of education, and in the latter part of the century Americans served as advisers to the Japanese Foreign Office. The Japanese, for their part, were generally deeply appreciative of the friendliness and spirit of justice characteristically manifested by the United States, particularly during the period of the anti-foreign outbreaks when armed aggression on the part of the great powers was a real probability.   In short, the period from 1868 (and it might even be dated from 1854) to the end of the nineteenth century was truly characterized by almost model cordiality as far as Japanese-American relations are concerned.   How and why these excellent relations came to deteriorate, ultimately leading to a great and bitter war in the Pacific, is told in subsequent chapters.

CHAPTER IV

THE BEGINNINGS OF MISUNDERSTANDINGS AND DIPLOMATIC STRIFE

SEETHING EAST ASIA

Swift developments in East Asia followed the conclusion of the Treaty of Shimonoseki between Japan and China. The decisiveness of the Japanese victory and the provision of the Shimonoseki treaty which gave Japan the Liaotung peninsula, and hence a foothold on the Asiatic mainland, greatly disturbed Russia, which at this time was resuming its aggressive expansion in the Far East. To the Russians, Japanese entrenchment in southern Manchuria would represent a deterrent to their aggressive designs. Consequently Russia took the lead in organizing a tripower intervention, supported by France and Germany, in which the three powers individually " advised " Japan to restore the Liaotung peninsula to China. The Russian note, a masterpiece of duplicity, pointed out that the Japanese retention of the Liaotung peninsula would be a constant menace to Peking, render illusory the independence of Korea, and therefore be a " perpetual obstacle to the permanent peace of the Far East." In this note the Czar professed to give proof of his friendship for the Japanese by " advising them to renounce the definitive possession of the peninsula."[1]

Without an ally, and keenly aware that refusal to accept the

" advice " might lead to grave complications with the three intervening powers, Japan had no alternative but to retrocede the peninsula. Although Japan was partly compensated by a small increase in the indemnity which China was to pay, this was small consolation for the Japanese and they held the Russians chiefly accountable for depriving them of the full fruits of victory. The Russian duplicity was, moreover, fully disclosed only three years later when they obtained a leasehold over Port Arthur and the Liaotung peninsula. This development of course greatly embittered the Japanese, and it must be regarded as a significant factor in the war that subsequently broke out between Japan and Russia.

As an aftermath of the Sino-Japanese War, which fully punctured any remaining illusions concerning the latent might of China, the more aggressive Western powers engaged in a mad scramble for concessions which lasted until 1899. In this reckless scramble Russia, Great Britain, France and Germany compelled China to concede a number of leaseholds and spheres of interest. Not to be outdone by its European models, Japan also secured a concession, namely a sphere of interest in Fukien province. Fearing that these concessions might result in the concessionaires discriminating against American commercial interests in the area under their control or influence, Secretary of State John Hay in 1898 issued his famous Open Door note. In substance this circular note asked each of the powers to respect the principal of the Open Door by not discriminating against or interfering with the equal rights of other powers in their particular leaseholds, concessions, or spheres of interest. It is to be noted that this John Hay note was not altruistic in intent and that it was not primarily concerned with the preservation of the territorial and administrative entity of China. On the contrary, it was essentially concerned with preserving all American treaty rights.

In the summer of 1900 a serious anti-foreign outbreak occurred in northern China, known as the Boxer Rebellion. Ostensibly it was an uprising fomented by secret Chinese societies, but actually it was encouraged by the ultra-conservative imperial government of China.   A joint allied expedition, including troops from Japan, finally succeeded in quelling the uprising, and in the Boxer Protocol, concluded in September between the foreign powers and the Chinese imperial government, China was saddled with a huge indemnity of $333,000,000 and required to furnish a number of guarantees for the safety of foreigners residing in China.

During the course of this rebellion it became very apparent that Russia might exploit the confused situation to further despoil China.   Accordingly, Secretary Hay in July 1900 issued his second circular note to each of the great powers.   In this note the scope of the first note was greatly expanded inasmuch as each of the great powers was asked to respect the territorial and administrative entity of China.   The policies and principles enunciated in the two notes, however, fundamentally represented American ideals and hopes rather than formal commitments on the part of the great powers.

THE RUSSO-JAPANESE WAR

The determination of Russia to secure hegemony over Manchuria, together with her persistent efforts since 1895 to maneuver into a position of primacy in Korea and displace the Japanese, created a dangerous tension between Japan and Russia.   Japan was now conscious of her newly found military power, and Korea had for years been regarded as of vital importance to the defense of the Japanese islands.   The possession of Korea by a great power such as Russia, or the establishment of military bases there, were considered grave threats.   Moreover, the Japanese had already developed extensive economic interests in Korea, and even Manchuria was regarded as an area of inevitable future economic expansion.   Russian domination of Korea and Russian preemption in Manchuria were consequently regarded as intolerable by the Japanese.

The Japanese knew that none of the great Western powers were very much interested in Korea.   They also knew that while the United States might fear Russian expansionism in the Far East and might indulge in high-sounding phrases about the Open Door and the territorial and administrative entity of China, neither the United States nor any other Western power could be counted on to implement the phrases with force if necessary. As early as 1901 Secretary Hay had in effect informed Japan that the United States was not then prepared " to attempt singly, or in concert with other powers, to enforce these views in the East by any demonstration which could present a character of hostility to any other power."[2]

After the Boxer Rebellion, Japan came to be regarded by both the United States and Great Britain as the one nation in a position to check Russia and thereby preserve the peace in East Asia. Since 1895 Great Britain had been cultivating Japan as a posssible ally to be used for the purpose of containing Russia and accordingly contributing to the security of India, which was then the heart of the far-flung British Empire. The Japanese on their part had been toying with the alternatives of a rapprochement with Russia or an alliance with Britain. The community of British and Japanese interests finally made possible the Anglo-Japanese Alliance, concluded in January 1902 for the stated purpose of preserving the status quo and the peace in the Far East and for the unstated purpose of specifically containing Russia. The agreement clearly implied that in case Russia became involved in war with Japan and were assisted by a third power, Britain would enter the war as an ally of Japan. This alliance enabled Japan to stiffen her policy against Russia.

After having exhausted the possibility of resolving by diplomacy the critical issues with Russia, and having failed largely because of the bad faith of Russia, Japan on January 6, 1904 broke off diplomatic relations. Two days later the Japanese launched a surprise attack on Port Arthur which inflicted considerabled damage. To the amazement of the Western world, which viewed the ensuing war as a conflict between a colossus and a mere dwarf, the Japanese won a series of sensational victories which culminated in the decisive victory at Mukden in March 1905. Two months later Admiral Togo practically annihilated a huge Russian fleet in the historic Battle of Tsushima Strait, one of the greatest naval engagements of modern times.

Despite these victories the Japanese armies had paid heavily in casualties and the Japanese military command was dubious of the ability of their exhausted armies to pursue the Russians deeper into northern Manchuria and into Siberia. On the domestic front the war effort had imposed a severe strain on the Japanese economy and there was evidence of its possible collapse if the war were further prolonged. Moreover, Germany and France were manifesting increasing hostility toward Japan. For all these reasons, the Japanese Government formally requested President Theodore Roosevelt in May 1905 to accept the role of mediator. This role Roosevelt was willing and eager to assume. Although revolution had broken out in European Russia, partly as a consequence of the military disasters in the Far East but principally because of political and social abuses of long standing which the people could no longer tolerate, the Russian Government on June 6 finally agreed to discuss peace, but with great reluctance because of the conviction that the war could still be won. On June 7 Roosevelt extended invitations to the belligerents to convene in Washington in August, but because of the intense summer heat in that city the discussions were transferred to Portsmouth, New Hampshire.

THE UNITED STATES AND THE WAR

When the Russo-Japanese War had broken out the sympathies of President Roosevelt and most Americans were with the Japanese whom they regarded as the underdogs. But there was a much more practical reason for this American sympathy. Aggressive Russia had for many years been regarded as the chief threat to the integrity of China and the Open Door principle. Russia had in effect engaged in a rather consistent diplomacy of cunning and deceit; and Hay, for example, had concluded that it was impossible to deal with the Russians, with whom "mendacity is a science." Quite justifiably Japan in those days was looked upon as a nation that was needed to check Russia and supply a sorely required stabilizing force in East Asia. The American press as a whole was very partial to Japan, and the influential *Journal of Commerce* confidently contended that Japan was fighting the battle of civilization and of equality of commercial opportunity in China. It is probable that Roosevelt was not displeased by Japan's resort to war against Russia, for immediately after the surprise attack on Port Arthur he argued that " Japan is playing our game."[3] Of more practical value to Japan than the expressions of sympathy and encouragement was the financial assistance of American bankers who cooperated with British bankers to supply the funds Japan needed to finance the war effort.[4]

Throughout the war the United States appeared to be primarily interested in safeguarding the principle of the Open Door and in preserving the territorial and administrative entity of China. On February 10, 1904, the very day on which Japan officially declared war, President Roosevelt in identical notes asked the two belligerents to respect "the neutrality of China and in all practicable ways her administrative entity."[5] No mention was made of Korea, although it was known that Japanese armies would rapidly overrun that country. At any rate, Russia refused to agree to the neutralization of Manchuria, and both Japan and Russia made their acceptance of the proposals dependent on acceptance by the other. Hay nevertheless again presumptiously announced that both nations had given assurances. Hay notwithstanding, both belligerents proceeded to violate the neutrality of China and used Manchuria for troop movements and actual fighting. Despite these not surprising developments, Hay on January 13, 1905 again circularized the principal powers to the effect that it was the policy of the United States to maintain the " integrity of China and the ' Open Door ' in the Orient." All the circularized powers gave satisfactory replies to the note, except Russia which insisted that the neutrality of China would be " considered from the standpoint of its own interest." Shortly after Roosevelt had agreed to act as mediator, he obtained from the Japanese Government a pledge that " Japan adheres to the position of maintaining the Open Door in Manchuria and of restoring that province to China." Such, in brief, were the Open Door pledges made during the war: Russia vacillated and equivocated, Japan finally gave firm assurances.

THE TREATY OF PORTSMOUTH

The peace conference convened in Portsmouth on August 9, 1905 and was in session less than a month. By this time most Americans had lost their earlier fervor for the righteousness of Japan's motives. Although her armies were temporarily exhausted and her economy was creaking from the strain of the war effort, Japan was nevertheless in a very advantageous position in the Far East and the Japanese Foreign Office naturally hoped to make the most of it. Roosevelt now became greatly concerned about the security of the Philippines and was anxious to establish some kind of a balance of power in the Far East. At this time, also, immigration troubles on the West Coast were embittering many Americans and giving rise to a growing Japanophobia. Roosevelt had actually only wanted to see Japan check Russia; he had not foreseen so drastic a defeat of the Russians. At the conference, and after, he therefore strove to restore a balance of power between Russia and Japan.[6] While his former partiality for Japan now cooled off perceptibly, it would be very incorrect to assume that he had become calculatingly hostile to Japan.

At the conference Roosevelt exerted his influence to tone down Japan's demands and to prevent her from becoming too powerful in the Far East. The Japanese initially demanded all of the island of Sakhalin and a huge indemnity of $600,000,000. Russia adamantly refused to yield to these demands, and Roosevelt intervened to bring about Japan's abandonment of claims for any indemnity and acceptance of the southern half of Sakhalin in lieu of the whole island. With the indemnity question out of the way, the Russians and Japanese were able to come to final terms, and the treaty, known as the Treaty of Portsmouth, was signed on September 5, 1905. It provided that Russia was to recognize the paramount interest of Japan in Korea, that the Liaotung peninsula was to be ceded to Japan, that all Russian mining and railroad concessions in southern Manchuria were to be transferred to Japan,* and that both Russia and Japan were to evacuate their troops from Manchuria and restore exclusive administration of that area to China. In addition, Russia was to cede to Japan the southern half of the island of Sakhalin.

While the treaty was very advantageous to Japan and actually gave her a preponderant position in East Asia, many Japanese were embittered by its terms and felt that Roosevelt had deprived them of the full fruits of victory. While this was the feeling of many zealots, it is very likely that the political and military leaders were reasonably satisfied that Japan had more than won the peace. For his efforts, Roosevelt was awarded the Nobel Prize for peace.

THE JAPANESE ANNEXATION OF KOREA

After the outbreak of the Russo-Japanese War, Japan moved swiftly to obtain complete control over Korea, realizing that such action would encounter no opposition from any of the powers except Russia, with whom she was at war anyway. Less than two weeks after the outbreak of the war, Japan negotiated an agreement with the Korean Government in which she guaranteed the independence and territorial entity of the country and promised

---

* The railroad from Changchun to Port Arthur and its branches was renamed by the Japanese the South Manchurian Railroad Company and was operated by a quasi-governmental company. The South Manchurian Railroad Company rapidly developed an extensive commercial empire in southern Manchuria.

protection for the royal family. After the conclusion of the war
with Russia, Japan in November 1905 established a virtual protectorate over the country.   Appeals of the Korean Emperor to
President Roosevelt were in vain, and Roosevelt took the position
that Korea " had shown herself utterly impotent either for self-
government or for self-defense."[7]   With Korea abandoned by
Roosevelt, who had written off the country for the security of the
Philippines, Japan took the final step and transformed Korea into
an integral part of the Japanese Empire.   In a treaty of August
1910 the friendless Korean Emperor ceded his rights of sovereignty
to the Emperor of Japan.[8]

Immediately prior to the conclusion of the Treaty of Portsmouth, William Howard Taft, who was then Secretary of War,
had concluded a secret agreement on July 29, 1905 with the Japanese Foreign Minister Katsura in which the United States recognized Japan's " sovereignty over Korea " and Japan in return
disclaimed any aggressive designs on the Philippine Islands.
Roosevelt reasoned that Japan's victory over Russia had placed
her in a predominant position in the Far East and that as a consequence the Philippine Islands were indefensible. He considered it expedient and wise to " barter " Korea, which was already in Japan's physical possession, for a Japanese guarantee not
to attack the Philippines.

Two months after the conclusion of the Treaty of Portsmouth,
the State Department obligingly withdrew all diplomatic representatives from Korea.   This was recognition of the fact that
Korea had become a Japanese dependency, and the action did
much to tone down Japanese resentment against Roosevelt for
having allegedly deprived Japan of all that was due her at Portsmouth.   On the other hand, many Korean patriots were bitterly
disappointed and felt that the United States had betrayed them.
When the Japanese Government formally annexed Korea by imperial decree, the State Department graciously recognized the
action promptly.   Thereafter the Japanese proceeded to under-
take a noteworthy economic development of the country, but at

the expense of the civil liberties of the Korean people, their nationalistic sensibilities, and their inalienable right to rule themselves. Despite the material gains of the Japanese administration, the Korean people maintained a sullen, passive resistance which occasionally manifested itself in outbreaks and unrest that were ruthlessly quashed. A Korean independence movement was established abroad, which kept up a constant agitation for the country's independence, but it did not receive any official encouragement from the United States until after the Japanese attack on Pearl Harbor in December 1941.

AN ERA OF STRAINED RELATIONS

The Treaty of Portsmouth marked a turning point in the history of American relations with Japan. American relations with Japan had been almost consistently cordial, but beginning with the Portsmouth peace conference, suspicion and antagonism manifested themselves and became more pronounced with the passing years. The principal underlying factor in this deterioration of relations was the rise of the United States as a world power with Far Eastern interests that clashed with those of Japan. More specific factors were the increasing efforts of the Japanese to consolidate their economic position in southern Manchuria, the American fear of rising Japanese naval power, American concern for the security of the Philippine Islands, and the advent of a grave immigration issue.

By the beginning of the twentieth century Japanese immigrants had displaced the Chinese as the most serious oriental immigration problem in America, despite the fact that the Japanese Government had consistently discouraged the emigration of Japanese nationals to the United States and other countries where they were not welcome. A treaty of 1894 between the United States and Japan provided for the unrestricted entry of Japanese nationals but reserved for the United States the right of domestic control over all immigrant laborers. Japanese immigration was heaviest in the Hawaiian Islands, and large numbers of Japanese nationals subsequently entered the United States from these islands. Notwithstanding the exaggerated outbursts of Californians and others about the possibility of being overwhelmed by the so-called Yellow wave, the number of Japanese in the United States was very small. The census of 1900 indicated 24,326 Japanese, and that of 1910 only 72,157.[9] By 1920 the total number of Japanese had declined to less than 72,000.

Nevertheless, by 1905 there had developed considerable animosity toward the Japanese on the West Coast, where they were proving themselves extremely successful as agriculturists and small business men. Popular hostility on the West Coast was largely based on the thin argument that the Japanese worked for lower wages and therefore endangered the standard of living of the native Americans. In 1906 Japanese immigrants became an international issue when the San Francisco school board callously ordered the segregation of all oriental school children, including 93 Japanese students. This action was most regrettable, for the Japanese Red Cross only a few months previously had contributed $244,960 to the victims of the great San Francisco earthquake and fire. This sum was larger than the contributions made by the rest of the world, excluding of course the United States.[10]

The Japanese press reacted to the school board's discriminatory action with mingled feelings of hurt and indignation. Alarmed and angered by the school board's action, President Roosevelt sent a personal representative to San Francisco to make an on-the-spot investigation, and he confided to his son Kermit that he was " horribly bothered about the Japanese business." In his annual message of December 1906 to the Congress, Roosevelt condemned the action of the school board as " wicked absurdity " and hinted that the Government might be compelled to take some kind of corrective action. Roosevelt then turned to " domestic diplomacy " and invited the members of the school board to Washington at government expense for a discussion of the problem. In Washington the members of the school board were shown " the sights " and assured by Roosevelt that the Government would solve the immigration problem by diplomatic means. On their return to San Francisco the members of the school board rescinded the obnoxious segregation order.

In a series of diplomatic exchanges in 1907 and 1908 by the American and Japanese governments, the immigration issue was equitably settled, temporarily at least, by the so-called Gentlemen's Agreement. In this agreement Japan pledged that she would not object to the exclusion of Japanese nationals seeking entry to the United States from Hawaii or other regions adjacent to the United States, such as Mexico and Canada, and that she would continue her policy of not issuing passports to laborers desiring to emigrate directly from Japan to the United States. In other words, the United States would not by statute exclude Japanese immigrants desiring to enter the country directly from Japan, and the Japanese Government would voluntarily deny permission for such emigration. Japan faithfully kept her pledged word, and the emigration of Japanese laborers to America came to a complete halt. Not only were no Japanese laborers given passports to emigrate to the United States, but, although not required to do so by the agreement, passports were also denied laborers wishing to emigrate to Hawaii.

While anxious to maintain the most cordial relations possible with Japan and to avoid all unnecessary offense to her, Roosevelt was also determined that no one in Japan would misinterpret his actions as stemming from any fear of Japanese power. In this respect he confided in July 1907 to his friend Henry White that he was " exceedingly anxious to impress upon the Japanese that I have nothing but the friendliest intentions toward them, but I am none the less anxious that they should realize I am not afraid of them."[11] To appreciate the significance of these feelings, it should be realized that at this time there was a great deal of irresponsible talk in the United States, particularly on the West Coast, of a possible war with Japan.

To impress the Japanese in particular, and the world in general, with the extent of the newly developed American naval might, Roosevelt hit upon the idea of ordering the U.S. battleship fleet on a round-the-world cruise. The fleet departed in December from Hampton Roads, Virginia, to the consternation of the Atlantic seaboard states which were thereby left undefended from a possible naval attack and to the glee of the Japanophobes on the West Coast and elsewhere who hoped that the fleet's departure presaged some kind of hostile action against Japan. The fleet rounded Cape Horn and received an enthusiastic welcome at several South American ports. On the invitation of the Japanese Government the fleet stopped at Yokohama, where it received one of its warmest welcomes, as school children lined the streets waving American flags. The fleet then resumed its cruise through the Indian Ocean, through the Suez Canal to Mediterranean ports, and then finally returned home on February 22, 1909, without a mishap, to the relief of all the Atlantic seaboard states.

The successful cruise whipped up American national pride and also impressed the whole world, not merely Japan, with the naval might of the United States, which now ranked second only to that of Great Britain. The successful cruise also served to add a final touch of the grandiose and flamboyant to the administration of Roosevelt, who retired from the presidency only a few days after the completion of the cruise.

In 1908, while the United States fleet was on its world cruise, Roosevelt had been instrumental in concluding an understanding with Japan of great significance. On November 30 of that year Secretary of State Root and the Japanese Ambassador in Washington, Baron Kogoro Takahira, concluded an agreement based on an exchange of notes, known as the Root-Takahira Agreement. This agreement was an executive commitment, not a treaty, and hence was technically binding only on the Roosevelt Administration which had negotiated it. In this agreement the United States and Japan pledged to preserve the status quo in the Pacific and to respect each other's territorial possessions there, to maintain the territorial integrity and independence of China, and to safeguard the common interests of all powers in China on the basis of the Open Door principle. The agreement also provided that in case any event arose to disturb the status quo in the Far East, the two powers would consult on measures to be taken.

Keenly aware of the dominant position of Japan in the Far East and the military weakness of the United States in that area, Roosevelt had evidently been prepared to give Japan a free hand in southern Manchuria in exchange for effective guarantees respecting the inviolability of the Philippines. His successor in the White House, William Howard Taft, differed with him on the necessity and wisdom of a strategic retreat from the advanced position that had been taken on Far Eastern policy. Instead of acquiescing to Japan's apparent policy of transforming southern Manchuria into an exclusive Japanese economic preserve, Taft insisted on the full application of the Open Door principle there and the right of Americans to participate on equal terms in that region's economic development.

Taft inaugurated a general policy known as " dollar diplomacy," which has often been misunderstood. Taft's " dollar diplomacy " aimed to protect and encourage American investments abroad, in the Far East as well as in the Caribbean area. As Taft explained it, dollars were to be substituted for bullets and it was a policy that appealed " alike to idealistic humanitarian sentiments, to the dictates of sound policy and strategy, and to legitimate commercial aims."[12]

In the Far East, Taft and his Secretary of State, Philander C. Knox, aggressively encouraged American bankers to take an active interest in Manchuria, particularly in the financing of railroad projects there. Taft believed that the financial activities of American bankers in Manchuria, backed by the State Department, would enhance the diplomatic position of the United States. In a memorandum to Secretary Knox he contended that " the nations that finance the great Chinese railroads and other enterprises will be foremost in the affairs of China and the participation of American capital in these investments will give the voice of the

United States more authority in political controversies in that country which will go far toward guaranteeing the preservation of the administrative entity of China." Unfortunately for Taft, however, American bankers did not have the slightest enthusiasm for financial adventures in Manchuria and the State Department practically had to force them to venture there.[13]

Late in 1909 Secretary Knox proposed to the great powers that an international group of bankers should jointly lend China enough money to buy all foreign-owned railroads in Manchuria, which would be operated by an international board until China could repay the loans in full.[14] This is known as the "Knox Neutralization Plan," and it obviously was an attempt to "smoke" Japan out of Manchuria. Both Russia and Japan* were hostile to the proposal, and Great Britain took the side of Japan, with whom she had concluded a hard and fast military alliance in 1905. The plan was consequently abandoned.

In 1911 a consortium consisting of British, German, French, Russian, Japanese and American bankers was organized for the purpose of making joint loans to the Chinese Government without any political significance. Even the consortium was a failure. It lent China only £27,000,000, of which American bankers advanced but $7,299,000.

Dollar diplomacy was a dismal failure in China. It actually accomplished one important, and undesirable, result: it drove Japan and Russia into closer relations and undid much that Theodore Roosevelt had done to improve Japanese-American relations. In a letter of December 22, 1910 Roosevelt had impatiently warned Taft that his China policy was largely bluff and one which could not be backed up if challenged by Japan. "As regards Manchuria," he wrote, "if the Japanese choose to follow a course of conduct to which we are adverse, we cannot stop it

---

* After the conclusion of the Treaty of Portsmouth, Japan and Russia gradually arrived at an understanding concerning their respective spheres of interest in Manchuria, with Japan to have southern Manchuria and Russia to have northern Manchuria.

unless we are prepared to go to war, and a successful war about Manchuria would require a fleet as good as that of England, plus an army as good as that of Germany."[15] Shortly after delivering his inaugural address of March 1913, President Wilson withdrew all government support from American banking activities in the Far East. Dollar diplomacy was over in the Far East.

Meanwhile, the immigration question had again risen to plague Japanese-American relations. As a result of pressure from anti-Japanese elements, the California legislature in 1913 prohibited aliens ineligible for citizenship to own land.* While the Japanese were not mentioned by name, this action was clearly directed against them and aroused bitter feelings in Japan. Secretary of State Bryan had made a futile trip to California in an effort to forestall passage of the law. In 1917 the immigration problem was further aggravated when the people of California voted, by means of the " initiative," to forbid aliens ineligible for citizenship to even lease land. And in 1924, seemingly in contempt of all that had been done in a statesmanlike manner to respect the sensitive feelings of orientals, the Congress passed a law which prohibited aliens ineligible for citizenship from entering the country. This was blunt exclusion and discrimination, and the action cut deeply into the sensitivities of the Japanese. Even the Secretary of State, Charles Evans Hughes, regretted the measure, and he felt that effective exclusion could have been obtained in a more subtle way by placing Japanese immigration on a quota basis, like that in effect for European immigration, since the Japanese population in the United States was numerically insignificant. Actually, on the quota system then in effect, only about a hundred Japanese would have been permitted to enter the country annually.

---

* In accordance with the law of America at that time, orientals born in Asiatic countries were ineligible for citizenship.

PROBLEMS ARISING FROM JAPAN'S ENTRANCE IN WORLD WAR I

With the outbreak of World War I early in August 1914, Japan was bound to give Great Britain assistance by virtue of the treaty of alliance which had been concluded in 1902 and renewed in 1905 and 1911. On August 15 Japan accordingly delivered an ultimatum to Germany demanding the surrender of her Tsingtao leasehold to Japan, who pledged ultimately to restore it to China. In taking this action the Japanese were doubtlessly as much motivated by the lure of fishing in the troubled waters of China as by the desire to honor the letter of the treaty of alliance with Great Britain. Since all the great European powers were involved in the war almost from its beginning, it was but natural that chauvinistic Japanese should relish the opportunity of stepping into the great political vacuum created by the withdrawal of the European powers, who now found it necessary to concentrate all their resources and armed power on the European struggle. With the failure of Germany to reply to the Japanese ultimatum, Japan promptly launched offensive operations with some 20,000 troops, aided by small contingents of British and Sikh forces. Tsingtao fell on November 7, and all German properties in the Shantung peninsula were seized, including the valuable Tsinan-Tsingtao railroad. The Chinese Government then requested the Japanese to withdraw from the railroad zone. The Japanese bluntly refused to comply with the request and made it clear that they would not retire from any part of the Shantung peninsula until the European war was over. The Japanese also seized the German islands north of the equator.

Taking full advantage of the preoccupation of the great powers in the European holocaust, the Japanese Government in January 1915 served on China a secret ultimatum, known as the Twenty-One Demands, which if entirely accepted would have transformed China into a Japanese protectorate. Although the ultimatum was intended to remain secret, the State Department soon learned of its extreme nature, and on March 13 Secretary Bryan informed Japan that the Twenty-One Demands could not be reconciled with the pledges which the principal powers, including Japan, had made to recognize the sovereignty of China. He added, however, that while the United States could not be indifferent to the efforts of any power to acquire domination over China, it nevertheless recognized that " territorial contiguity creates special relations " and that Japan consequently possessed special relations with Manchuria, eastern Inner Mongolia and Shantung.[16] This note obviously represented an attempt by Bryan to reconcile Japan's demands with traditional American policy in the Far East, and in a very real sense it was a significant retreat from the precarious policy that had been established by Taft to deprive Japan of any special rights in any part of China, including southern Manchuria.

Yielding somewhat to the diplomatic pressure of the United States, Japan toned down the demands which she presented in a final ultimatum to China on May 7. The final Twenty-One Demands comprised five groups. The first four groups required China to concede to Japan the economic domination of Shantung, southern Manchuria and eastern Inner Mongolia; to agree to joint Sino-Japanese control of the valuable Han Yeh-ping iron mines near Hankow; and to pledge not to alienate to any third power any bay or harbor along the entire Chinese coast. The fifth group of demands provided for the acceptance of Japanese advisers, joint control of the munitions industry, and joint administration of police functions in certain strategic areas. This group, if accepted, would have transformed China into a Japanese dependency and puppet.

Four days after these demands had been presented to China, again in the form of an ultimatum, Secretary Bryan informed Japan that the United States could not accept any agreement made by Japan and China " impairing the treaty rights of the United States or its citizens in China, the political or territorial integrity of the Republic of China or the international policy . . .

commonly known as the open door policy."[17] That is to say, the United States would not recognize any changes brought about under duress which violated existing international understandings. In a sense, then, this statement was a forerunner of the later policy advanced by Secretary of State Stimson of non-recognition of changes brought about through the use of force.

Thanks to the diplomatic support of the United States, moderate as it was, the helpless and insecure Chinese Government was able to procrastinate and secure a mitigation of the original severity of the demands. In two treaties and subsequent agreements China complied with most of the demands of the first four groups, but group five was put off and finally withdrawn by Japan.

Having acquired a dominant position in China as a result of the agreements exacted from China under duress, Japan now strove to obtain wider recognition of this privileged position.[18] In February 1917 the British Ambassador in Tokyo secretly pledged that Britain would support Japan's claims to former German rights in Shantung and to possession of the former German islands north of the equator. In the same year France and Russia made similar secret pledges in support of Japanese claims.

On April 6, 1917 the United States entered the war on the side of the Allies as an " associated power." President Wilson immediately strove to transform the great struggle of power politics into one of ideology, with democracy ostensibly seeking to destroy the forces of autocracy and militarism. Since the arrangements made by Japan for territorial acquisitions had been secretly made and the United States had not been officially informed of them, Wilson took the position that he did not know about them. This of course was casuistry.

On August 14 China also entered the war, not by action of parliament or the will of the people, but by the action of the militarists who had seized control of the government. Whereas Japan played a very important part in the war by providing extensive naval operations, not to mention the military operations in the Far East, China was able to offer little more than an army of coolies who labored behind the lines in France. Nevertheless, by virtue of having formally entered the war China was as entitled as Japan to sit in at the peace conference which would be convoked with the termination of the conflict.

THE LANSING-ISHII AGREEMENT

In 1917 Japan made a strenuous diplomatic effort to obtain the acquiescence of the United States to the privileged position she had obtained in China as a result of the agreements that had been wrung from the Chinese Government in 1915 and the confirmations that had been secured in secret understandings with Great Britain, France and Russia in early 1917. In the summer of that year the crack diplomat, Viscount Kikujiro Ishii, was sent to Washington in an attempt to reconcile Japanese and American differences and remove American objections to the privileged position that had been obtained in China. During the conversations with Secretary Lansing, Ishii insisted on American recognition of the special interests of Japan in China, while Lansing, who had displaced Bryan as Secretary of State, insisted on a Japanese reaffirmation of the principles of the integrity of China and the Open Door. A compromise was effected in a public exchange of notes on November 2, 1917, known as the Lansing-Ishii Agreement.

In this agreement it was again recognized that " territorial propinquity creates special relations between countries, and consequently the government of the United States recognizes that Japan has special interests in China, particularly in parts to which her possessions are contiguous." The phrase " particularly in parts to which her possessions are contiguous " was an obvious reference to southern Manchuria. In the agreement it was further understood that the principles of the territorial integrity of China and the Open Door were to remain unimpaired and that neither country would attempt to secure privileges which would violate these principles.[19]

In a sense, the Lansing-Ishii Agreement recognized that the spirit of the Monroe Doctrine was to apply to the Far East, with Japan assuming there a role similar to that played by the United States in the Western Hemisphere. For practical reasons, however, the agreement was obviously vague and only as effective in promoting peace and stability in China as the spirit of the nations entering into it. The agreement nevertheless contributed toward halting the worsening of Japanese-American relations which had been underway since Taft had attempted to carry out the policy of dollar diplomacy in the Far East.

VERSAILLES AND THE FAR EAST

The peace conference convened in Paris on January 18, 1919. Present at the opening session were seventy delegates representing twenty-seven of the victorious nations. Russia, of course, was not represented, as the Bolshevists had seized power in 1917 and made a separate peace with Germany in March of the following year. The principal business of the conference was the settlement of European problems arising from the war. Far Eastern problems were of minor concern, except for the Japanese and Chinese delegates. While the victorious allied nations appeared to be primarily interested in the spoils of victory, President Wilson the idealist was more interested in the conclusion of a just peace and the establishment of a permanent organization for the promotion of world peace, namely the League of Nations. Only by agreeing to a number of compromises and concessions which violated his high ideals was Wilson able to win the adherence of the victorious powers to the establishment of the League and acceptance of its charter, or Covenant, as it was called. The United States, however, never became a member of the League, as the Senate considered membership in it a departure from traditional isolationist policy and an invitation to participate in world power politics and its endless wars.

The Japanese delegation of five was headed by Prince Saionji and Count Makino. It had very little interest in the European settlements and was mainly concerned with obtaining for Japan confirmation to title of the German properties seized in Shantung and the German islands north of the equator. The Japanese delegation felt that the claims of Japan were well buttressed as a result of the agreements of 1915 with China and the promises of support made in the secret treaties of 1917 with her principal European allies.

China had great difficulty in sending a suitable delegation, as the country was then split into two hostile factions, one governing from Canton and the other from Peking. A common delegation was finally agreed on, however, headed by Li Chen-hsiang. At the conference the Chinese delegation attempted to bring up the question of reexamination of all rights and privileges held by foreign powers in China that had been obtained under duress in the past. On this proposal the Chinese delegation was completely rebuffed, since the conference had been called to settle specific problems arising from the war rather than problems that had accrued in the preceding half century or more. The Chinese delegation also failed to win support for its contention that the agreements exacted in 1915 by Japan were invalid because they had been obtained under duress. On a third issue, the question of former German rights and properties in Shantung, the Chinese actually received considerable support, particularly from the American delegation. The Shantung question was finally settled as follows: Japan would retain possession of the former economic concessions and properties formerly held by the Germans, but on condition that at a proper time Shantung province would be restored to China. This settlement provoked bitter resentment in China, and the Chinese delegation refused to sign the finalized Treaty of Versailles.

On the question of the disposition of the former German islands in the Pacific, the Japanese delegation encountered considerable opposition from the American delegation, notwithstanding the pledges made in the secret treaties of 1917. However, since Australia and New Zealand put forth strenuous demands for the German islands south of the equator, the American delegation felt constrained to yield and compromise. It was finally decided to permit the Japanese to retain custody of the islands north of the equator under a so-called League of Nations Mandate. In accordance with this provision, the Japanese would not be granted outright and exclusive possession of the islands, but instead would act as a trustee in their administration for the League. The same arrangement was also made concerning the former German islands south of the equator, which passed under the trusteeship of Australia and New Zealand.

At the conference the Japanese delegation placed the Caucasian delegates in an embarrassing position when it proposed for inclusion in the Covenant of the League the principle of racial equality. The principle as proposed by the Japanese stipulated that: " The equality of nations being a basic principle of the League of Nations, the High Contracting Parties agree to accord, as soon as possible, to all aliens, nationals or states, making no distinction, either in law or in fact, on account of their race or nationality." The proposal had the support of Wilson, as well as of the French and Italian delegates. The British delegates were horrified, however, and exerted their powerful influence to have it defeated. Needless to say, the defeat of this proposal did not enhance the prestige of the Westerner in Asia.

THE SIBERIAN INTERVENTION

Following the overthrow of the Russian Government in November 1917 and the establishment of a Communist Government in Moscow, Siberia was plunged into a prolonged period of turmoil. During this period armies of so-called White Russians, bitterly opposed to Communism, attempted to destroy the Communist revolution and establish conservative forms of government. The question of Allied intervention in Siberia arose after March

1918, when Communist Russia concluded a separate peace with Germany and formally withdrew from the war. Allied intervention in Siberia was considered desirable for the following reasons: (1) stocks of war materials in Vladivostok and elsewhere, which had been supplied by the Allied nations, should be prevented from possibly falling into German hands; (2) a second front might be opened against Germany by driving westward across Siberia; and (3) assistance was needed by a Czechoslovak force of some fifty thousand men which was fighting its way across Siberia in the hope of reaching Vladivostok and then being transported to France for action against Germany.*

While the Western Allies were deliberating, Japan took the initiative and sent a force into Vladivostok on April 4. A small British force was also dispatched to Vladivostok. On July 2 the Allies finally agreed on a joint invasion of Siberia, primarily for the purpose of establishing a second front against Germany and forcing her to divert troops to the east. Not until July 17 did the United States agree to participate in the Siberian intervention, and it was carefully explained to the Allied nations that the objective of the American intervention was restricted to guarding the war material that had been supplied to Russia by the Allies and the United States.[20]

In implementation of the above decisions, British, Japanese, French and American troops were transported to Vladivostok between August and November. The Japanese force numbered more than 72,000, while the American force was limited to 9,000. The American force was under the command of Major General William S. Graves, who was instructed not to interfere in any way with the political sovereignty of Russia or her internal af-

---

* At that time most of Czechoslovakia was an unwilling and unhappy part of the Austro-Hungarian Empire. The Czechoslovak troops mentioned above had been drafted by Austria-Hungary for service on the eastern front and had been taken prisoners by Czarist Russia. With Russia now out of the war, they wanted to fight on the side of the Allies and contribute to the defeat of the Central Powers and the birth of a Czechoslovak state.

fairs.[21]   Graves adhered scrupulously to these instructions.

By the end of 1919 the Red armies had practically destroyed all the armies of counter-revolution and'had made the Communist state secure against all enemies.   This was significant, for, despite the official explanations of the Allied powers, many of their statesmen hoped to crush Communism by encouraging and assisting the counter-revolutionary forces.   Moreover, the German armies had laid down their arms in November 1918, and there now was no longer any defensible justification for continuation of the intervention.   Consequently Britain, France and the United States withdrew their forces from Siberia in 1920, but the Japanese troops remained until 1922.

Japanese troops had occupied the northern half of Sakhalin and were in possession of strategic points from Vladivostok to Chita. While the Japanese undoubtedly hoped to profit from the confused situation in Siberia, they were also motivated by a strong fear of Communism, particularly since Siberia was in close proximity to Japan and contiguous to Korea.   Apparently Japan hoped for the establishment of a buffer state in eastern Siberia which would be non-Communist, and some Japanese of influence advocated the annexation of the Maritime Province.

The continued presence of Japanese troops in Siberia played on the suspicions and distrust of many Americans and served to strain relations between Japan and the United States.   Finally realizing that the Siberian adventure was accomplishing nothing more than to increase the public debt and further to alienate the United States, the Japanese Government in 1922 ordered all troops withdrawn from Siberia.

CHAPTER V

THE WASHINGTON CONFERENCE AND THE QUEST FOR SECURITY

FACTORS RESPONSIBLE FOR THE CONFERENCE

Japan emerged from World War I in a position of entrenched hegemony in the Far East. The prolonged period of internal turmoil in Siberia and the military weakness of the Communist Government in Moscow had operated to reduce Russia to a political cypher in the Far East. The collapse of Russian power in the Far East had created a power vacuum which was filled by Japanese power and influence. Moreover, China with her sprawling land mass and huge population was without a central government whose authority was respected by the country as a whole, and individual warlords were operating like petty dictators. China had neither the unity nor the means to oppose Japanese power or to defend her outlying territories, particularly the rich and undeveloped region of Manchuria. Contrasting with this absence of a formidable military power on the continent, Japan possessed the world's third largest navy, a powerful land army, and a geographical position of great strategic advantage. No one in 1921 questioned that there was not a single power in a position to challenge Japan in the Far East by force of arms.

It was apparent to Secretary of State Hughes in 1921 that the position of Japan had become so enhanced as a result of the collapse of Russian Far Eastern power that the advanced position which the United States had been maintaining on the Open

Door policy since 1900 was no longer tenable as a unilateral American policy. Either the United States was to abandon its advanced interpretation of the Open Door policy or it was to be converted into a multilateral guarantee.

Both the United States and Japan were highly dependent on sea power for the support of their Far Eastern policies, the former because of its remoteness from the area and the latter because of her island nature. Manifestly, no political settlement could be made by the United States and Japan unless it were preceded or accompanied by a naval understanding of some kind.

As a result of the World War which had just been concluded, Great Britain, the United States and Japan had greatly expanded their navies. And although the war had ended and the enemy had been completely vanquished, each of these three powers was jealously engaging in a building program which aimed at naval hegemony in their respective areas of primary interest. In all these countries, however, and particularly in the United States and Great Britain, the people were chafing under the heavy financial burden of armaments and were looking to their leaders for the conclusion of some kind of a political settlement which would bring a halt to what appeared to be a dangerous and ruinous armaments race.

In response to the widespread demand of the American public for the reduction of naval armaments by treaty arrangement, Senator Borah early in 1921 introduced a resolution, endorsed by the Senate, which invited President Harding to summon the principal naval powers to a conference for the purpose of agreement on naval limitation. The resolution received House concurrence in June, and the President then instructed Secretary of State Hughes to make preparations for such a conference in Washington.[1] Because of the concommitant necessity of also settling Far Eastern political problems, all the powers, large and small, with Far Eastern interests were invited to participate in the conference. The following nations accepted invitations: Great Britain, Japan, France, Italy; and Portugal, the Netherlands, Belgium and China.

China was invited to participate largely in the hope that the presence of a Chinese delegation might serve as a restraining influence on the big powers in dealing with China problems.* The Soviet Union was not invited to participate, allegedly because she did not at the time possess vital Far Eastern interests,† but actually because of the fear of Communism and the refusal of the United States and the other powers to extend, even indirectly, any type of recognition to the outlawed Communist regime in Moscow.

ACCOMPLISHMENTS OF THE CONFERENCE

The Washington Conference convened on November 12, 1921 and adjourned early in February of the following year. During the three-month session the delegates reached agreements on the two major problems of naval limitation and Far Eastern political questions. Four important settlements were agreed on: (1) a Naval Limitation Treaty; (2) a Nine-Power Treaty, concerning China; (3) a Four-Power Treaty, concerning insular possessions in the Pacific; and (4) a Shantung understanding, concerning Japan and China.

The Naval Limitation Treaty was signed by Great Britain, the United States, Japan, France and Italy. It provided for a capital ship ratio of 5 : 5 : 3 : 1.75 : 1.75, with 525,000 gross tons established as the upper limit for the United States and Great Britain, and 315,000 gross tons for Japan. The signatories agreed to suspend their capital ship construction programs and to build new ships

---

* China at this time was in a chaotic condition, with a government in Peking that was not at all representative of the Chinese people as a whole, and a so-called Constitutionalist Government, of a revolutionary nature, in Canton headed by Dr. Sun Yat-sen. The invitation was sent to the Peking Government.

† Eastern Siberia was then governed by a so-called Far Eastern Republic, which was theoretically non-Communist but known to be linked to Moscow. Shortly after the convocation of the Washington Conference it voluntarily became a part of the Soviet Union.

only for the replacement of withdrawn ships. The agreement also provided that the respective powers would not fortify their island possessions in the Pacific area, except for specified exceptions, notably the Hawaiian Islands, Australia and New Zealand. The treaty was to remain in effect until the end of 1936, and a two-year notice was required for its abrogation.

The 5 : 5 ratio of equality between the United States and Great Britain applied to the fighting power of capital ships and absolute tonnage equality in aircraft carriers. While parity in other naval categories was not stipulated in the treaty, it was contended by American navy enthusiasts that it was implied as a result of certain public declarations made by British leaders prior to the convocation of the conference.[2] Even if it were so, this was small consolation to the American taxpayer, for the actual attainment of parity in all categories other than capital ships would have required an extensive naval construction program extending to 1942 because of the larger tonnage of such ships which Great Britain already had in actual service. Many Americans were consequently disappointed with the treaty because it had not granted the United States full parity with Great Britain either in theory or in actuality (without the need of costly construction).

The 5 : 3 ratio between the United States and Japan was considered satisfactory by the naval experts of both countries. The United States with a 5 : 3 ratio of capital ships, then the backbone of offensive power, could not successfully attack Japan. It was calculated that an attack on Japan would require a navy twice as large as the Japanese fleet. Conversely, Japan with a 3 : 5 ratio could not successfully attack either Hawaii or the United States. In other words, the naval treaty had reduced the navies of the three principal naval powers to defensive rather than offensive roles.

The second major agreement, the Nine-Power Treaty, was signed by all the powers participating in the conference. It solemnized in treaty form most of the substance of the Open Door policy that had been consistently advocated by the State Department, and it moreover made the preservation of the territorial integrity of China and the Open Door a multilateral obligation rather than a unilateral undertaking by the United States, as it had been in the past. The treaty specifically provided that all the contracting parties were to respect the sovereignty, independence and territorial and administrative integrity of China; that they were to maintain and advance the principle of equal commercial opportunity in China (the Open Door); and that they were not to take or support any action designed to establish spheres of interest or exclusive privileges in designated parts of China. This last provision was identical to the secret protocol of the Lansing-Ishii Agreement of 1917 to the effect that the contracting parties would " refrain from taking advantage of conditions in China in order to seek special rights which would abridge the rights of subjects or citizens of friendly states, and from countenancing action inimical to the security of those states."* The treaty also provided that Japan was to evacuate all troops from Siberia and that all the contracting parties would fully respect China's rights as a neutral power.

The Nine-Power Treaty contained a number of other provisions, some of which were in the nature of promises, such as to examine the problem of extraterritoriality in China, the withdrawal of foreign troops stationed in China, and the possible abandonment of leaseholds in China. Needless to say, China was greatly disappointed by the finalized treaty, for she had expected the powers to make extensive concessions in the surrendering of all extraterritorial and other privileges which compromised the full and complete independence of China.

In the third major agreement, the Four-Power Treaty, signed by Great Britain, the United States, Japan and France, the contracting parties agreed to respect the inviolability of each other's insular possessions in the Pacific area. They further pledged to settle by diplomacy any unforeseen disagreements or difficulties

---

* The Lansing-Ishii Agreement was subsequently abrogated.

arising among them concerning these possessions. As article 2 of the treaty put it, if the rights of any of the powers were threatened by the aggressive action of any other power, they were to " communicate with one another fully and frankly in order to arrive at an understanding as to the most effective measures to be taken, jointly or separately, to meet the exigencies of the particular situation." On paper, at least, the treaty brought into being a Pacific concert of the four greatest Far Eastern powers of that time. By this treaty Japan also pledged not to molest the Philippine Islands. This pledge was of some consolation to those Americans who feared that with only a 5:3 superiority in capital ships the United States navy could not successfully defend the Philippine Islands from a Japanese attack.

The fourth major settlement, the Shantung Agreement, was concluded by Japan and China in direct discussions, with British and American delegates sitting in as observers. By this agreement Japan pledged to restore to China the entire Shantung peninsula which she had occupied since 1914. Detailed arrangements for the application of all the provisions of the agreement were to be worked out subsequently in Tokyo by Chinese and Japanese diplomats. The Shantung problem was accordingly amicably settled in Tokyo, in the following year, and the stipulated transfers were carried out.

Mention might also be made of a minor treaty concluded between the United States and Japan which gave the United States the right to establish a submarine cable terminal on the island of Yap. This island had been mandated to Japan by the Treaty of Versailles.

While only a limited success, the Washington Conference nevertheless relieved the international tension and inaugurated a period of relative calm and mutual trust. The Naval Limitation Treaty and the Nine-Power and Four-Power treaties appeared to have stabilized the Far Eastern situation. The long period of suspicion and distrust between the United States and Japan seemed to have taken a definite turn for the better. In 1923 Japanese-American relations were further improved as a result of the generous philanthropic response of the American people to the victims of the disastrous Tokyo-Yokohama earthquake. Unfortunately, the Congress in the following year passed its notorious immigration act excluding all orientals, including the Japanese, and thereby with one stroke undid much that had been accomplished by diplomacy and philanthropy. Needless to say, this action of the Congress deeply offended the sensitive Japanese and played squarely into the hands of the militarists and ultranationalists who were chafing under the restrictions of the Washington treaties.

THE PACT OF PARIS

On a visit to France in the spring of 1927, Professor James T. Shotwell of Columbia University presented to Aristide Briand, the Foreign Minister of France, his ideas on a pact among nations to outlaw war as an instrument of national policy. Deeply enthused by the idea, Briand on April 6, 1927 informed the American people, through the Associated Press, that France was prepared to conclude an agreement with the United States renouncing war as an instrument of national policy which " would furnish the world the best illustration of the truth that the condition immediately to be obtained is not disarmament but the practice of peace."* There was no immediate reaction from the State Department, but on April 25 Nicholas Murray Butler, President of Columbia University, addressed a letter to the *New York Times* in which he urged the United States Government to accept the Briand proposal. Despite the apathy of Secretary of State Kellogg and the State Department, the National Grange, with some 800,000 members, endorsed a resolution prepared by Senator Borah which outlawed war as an instrument of national policy. By this time the press and the public were expressing such support of the

---

* .This was in line with the persistent policy of the French Government at that time that security should precede disarmament. This policy stemmed from the fear of a resurgent Germany.

proposal that the State Department could no longer remain impassive.

On June 20 Briand submitted to the United States Government a formal proposal for a bilateral pact of perpetual friendship based on a mutual pledge to condemn war as an instrument of national policy. Six months later Secretary Kellogg somewhat hesitantly informed the French Government that the United States was willing to conclude such a pact of peace provided other nations in addition to the United States and France would adhere to it. A number of nations immediately warmed up to this suggestion, and in August 1928 fifteen nations, including the United States, France, Great Britain, Japan, Italy, Russia and Germany, signed the pact of peace in Paris. Although unrecognized by the United States at that time, Russia was drawn into the pact by the good offices of France. By 1936 a total of 63 nations had signed the pact, and only five nations were then non-signatories, comprising Argentina, Bolivia, El Salvador, Uruguay and Yemen.

The Pact of Paris, also known as the Kellogg-Briand Pact, contained two pledges: (1) the contracting parties condemned recourse to war for the solution of international controversies and renounced it as an instrument of national policy, and (2) the contracting parties pledged to settle international disputes by pacific means. In his interpretative note of June 23 Secretary Kellogg stated that in signing the pact no nation surrendered its right to self-defense. "Every nation is free at all times," he asserted, "and regardless of treaty provisions, to defend its territory from attack or invasion and it alone is competent to decide whether the circumstances necessitate recourse to war in self-defense."[3]

In signing the pact each nation attached the reservation that a war of self-defense was not precluded; that it would be the judge of what constituted a war of self-defense; and that existing treaties were not to be impaired by the pledge. Great Britain attached the particular reservation that the pact did not prejudice her freedom of action in certain regions of the world which were vital to her peace and safety. The United States Senate, while not insisting on any reservations as such nevertheless interpreted the pact to mean that the United States did not renounce the right to wage war in self-defense or to " maintain the Monroe Doctrine, which is a part of our system of national defense." The Senate also made the interpretation that the contracting parties would not be bound to retaliate with punitive or coercive measures in case any signatory violated the pact.*

The common man throughout the world hailed the pact as the harbinger of a new era. The tranquil international situation and the manifestations of international good will at the time seemed to justify such hopes. However, some of the political and legal experts were not at all impressed. They contended that the pact was practically emasculated since it did not condemn all types of war, including wars of defense, and it provided no sanctions of any kind against aggressors. They argued that all nations in going to war have always insisted that they were fighting in self-defense. Senator Carter Glass of Virginia probably expressed the sentiments of most realistic Americans when he stated that although he intended to vote for the ratification of the pact, he was " not willing anybody in Virginia shall think I am simple enough to suppose that it is worth a postage stamp in the direction of accomplishing permanent international peace." Even Secretary Kellogg, one of the principal artificers of the pact, admitted that " the only enforcement behind the pact is the public opinion of people."

Manifestly the pact did not add anything to the League's provisions against aggression; actually it did not even go as far as the Covenant, which provided for possible punitive actions against aggressors. Moreover, the pact failed to provide any machinery for the settlement of disputes by pacific means. Nevertheless, President Hoover and Prime Minister Ramsay MacDonald

---

* These interpretations may be found in the report submitted to the Senate by its Committee on Foreign Relations.

of Great Britain in October 1929 announced that "both our governments resolve to accept the peace pact not only as a declaration of good intentions but as a positive obligation to direct national policy in accordance with its pledges."

The pact was subjected to its first test shortly after it was concluded. As a result of the Chinese seizure of the Chinese Eastern Railroad in Manchuria, which up to that time had been under joint Russo-Chinese control, the Soviet Union in July 1929 severed diplomatic relations with China. Hostilities then broke out and a small Russian force chastised a contingent of Chinese troops and disarmed ten thousand of them on Chinese soil. Fearing that serious consequences might result from this incident, Secretary of State Stimson took the lead in getting forty-two signatories of the Pact of Paris, including Japan and Germany, to remind both China and Russia of their obligations under the pact. Fortunately this disturbance was short-lived as a result of the conclusion of an understanding between Russia and China. For its efforts at peace-making the United States received a rebuke from the Soviet Government which described American diplomatic intervention as an unfriendly act and stated that "the Soviet government cannot forbear expressing amazement that the government of the United States, which by its own will has no official relations with the Soviet,* deems it possible to apply to it with advice and counsel." The incident clearly revealed that any single power which took the initiative in calling an apparent aggressor's attention to the obligations of the pact would incur the strong displeasure of the aggressor concerned.

As a result of Japan's invasion of Manchuria in 1931 and the fruitless effort of the United States to restrain her by diplomatic persuasion, Secretary Stimson in 1932 advanced the interpretation that the Pact of Paris altered the traditional concept of neutrality and that " a conflict becomes of concern to everybody connected

---

* It was not until 1933 that the Roosevelt administration extended de jure recognition to the Soviet Union.

with the Pact."[4] In 1934 the International Law Association, meeting in Budapest, interpreted the pact to mean that (1) a breach of the pact was a legal wrong not merely against the victim but against all signatories of the pact, and (2) the traditional law of neutrality was altered to permit a neutral nation to depart from a position of impartiality toward belligerents, whether aggressors or victims of aggression. Neither of these interpretations, however, could be considered a part of accepted international law, and many eminent authorities on international law, such as Prof. Borchard of Yale University, disagreed with them entirely.

Contemporaneously with the conclusion of the Pact of Paris, the State Department concluded a number of bilateral treaties with non-American nations which provided for the submission of justiciable disputes to The Hague Permanent Court of Arbitration or some other competent tribunal. In all these treaties, however, the Senate reserved the right to pass judgment on the nature and scope of each arbitration. Treaties of this nature were not, incidentally, concluded with Japan, Great Britain, Russia or Spain. A number of conciliation treaties were also concluded which provided for a " cooling off " period before any overt action of a military nature would be taken, during which period an effort would be made to find a formula for settling the dispute. No conciliation treaty was concluded with Japan.

THE FAILURE OF NAVAL LIMITATION

As has been indicated, the Washington Conference of 1921–22 ended on a note of harmony and hope for the future. It had apparently settled the disturbing political problems of the Far East and had established an equilibrium and clime in which the great powers could safeguard and promote their legitimate Pacific interests without the danger of incurring a general war. It had also made a beginning in the limitation of naval armaments by establishing a 5 : 5 : 3 ratio on capital ships for the three greatest naval powers.

By 1927 however the great naval powers had renewed the armaments race, particularly in the construction of cruisers, submarines and other categories not restricted by the Washington Naval Treaty. With the view of easing his country's tax burden as well as international tension, President Coolidge in February 1929 invited the principal naval powers to convene in Geneva for the specific purpose of extending the tonnage-limitation agreement. Only Great Britain and Japan accepted the invitation. France and Italy declined to attend on the ground of prior obligations to the League of Nation's own disarmament program, and they also contended that naval disarmament should not be treated separately but as an integral part of " whole " disarmament, including land and air disarmament.

Despite the absence of representatives from France and Italy, the conference met on June 20. It adjourned six weeks later, on August 4. Efforts of the United States to extend the 5 : 5 : 3 ratio to all categories of ships failed, principally because of the opposition of Great Britain. Britain was reluctant to abandon her supremacy of the seas, and she was willing to grant full parity to the United States only on condition that higher absolute tonnage limits would be established for each category of ships, which of course was frowned upon by the economy-minded Coolidge administration. The conference ended in complete failure.

The conclusion of the Pact of Paris in the following year appeared again to ease the rising international tension, and the moment seemed to be propitious for another and further attempt at naval disarmament. In 1929 the Prime Minister of Great Britain, Ramsay MacDonald, visited President Hoover in Washington, and they doubtless reached an understanding on the issue of Anglo-American naval parity. The way was now cleared for the summoning of another conference.

In January 1930 the five leading naval powers convened in London, under the auspices of the British Government. The conference lasted two months, and a naval treaty of considerable scope was signed by Great Britain, the United States, and Japan.

France and Italy, jealous of each other's naval power, subscribed only to minor clauses. The treaty provided for an upper limit in all categories of ships; a 10 : 10 : 6 ratio for capital ships and heavy cruisers, with a halt on capital ships construction; a 10 : 10 : 7 ratio for light cruisers and auxiliary craft; and parity for all powers on submarines, with an upper limit fixed at 52,700 gross tons. An " escalator," or escape, clause, inserted on the insistence of Great Britain, partly vitiated the agreement since it permitted any of the signatories to consider the ratios not binding if they felt their security was threatened by naval construction on the part of a non-signatory power.* The treaty was to remain in effect until the end of 1936, and provision was made for the summoning of another naval conference in 1935.

The Senate approved the treaty, 58–9, but only after a bitter debate which resulted in the passage of a resolution to the effect that the United States would not be bound by any secret understanding. It was erroneously believed that Hoover had authorized the American delegation to conclude some such understanding at the conference. The American public was in general disappointed with the treaty, inasmuch as it did not provide for reduction in naval armaments and instead extended a system of ratios to which the United States would have to build up because of Great Britain's greater existing tonnage. It was estimated that such a building program would cost the taxpayers about a billion dollars. This is a very small amount of money to spend today for armaments, but in those days of economy-mindedness it seemed like a staggering sum.

In June 1934 preliminary discussions took place in London concerning the next naval conference which was to be held in the following year as stipulated by the London Naval Treaty of 1930. The Japanese initially insisted on parity in all categories of ships, but later offered to agree to the abolition of capital ships, aircraft carriers and large cruisers, which they termed " offensive " types.

---

* At that time Great Britain was apprehensive of future German naval plans.

The American delegation was opposed to the suggestion. Disagreement also arose between the American and British delegations on the question of full parity in all categories for their respective countries. The conference was adjourned on December 19 on a note of discord. Ten days later Japan served the required two-year notice of her withdrawal from the obligations of both the Washington and London Naval treaties.[5] This meant that after December 1936 Japan would be free to carry out an unrestricted naval construction program. The Japanese action reflected the impotence of the civilian elements in Japan and the dominant control which the Army and Navy had obtained over the government.

Late in 1935 the five leading naval powers met in London in what proved to be the last international effort to limit naval armaments before the outbreak of World War II. Although Japan had denounced the Washington and London Naval treaties, she sent delegates to the conference on the urging of Great Britain. The respective delegations were far apart from the moment discussions began. The Japanese insistence on full naval parity with Great Britain and the United States was uncompromisingly opposed by the American delegation, chiefly on the ground that with two long coastlines to defend naval parity would mean naval inferiority for the United States. In January of the following year the Japanese delegation withdrew from the conference. Late in March the conference adjourned after an emasculated treaty was signed by Great Britain, the United States and France, which provided for certain qualitative limitations and a number of escape clauses. Italy failed to sign the treaty as a result of France's refusal to concede her naval parity.

With the failure of this naval conference the postwar effort at naval limitation was over. Each of the nations now embarked on an unrestricted naval building program. The era of suspicion, distrust and fear was fully underway. The doves of peace that had hovered in the sky for so many years now vanished from sight.

CHAPTER VI

THE FATEFUL DECADE, 1931-1941

THE INVASION OF MANCHURIA

Following the death of Sun Yat-sen in 1924, leadership of the Kuomintang, or Nationalist Party, of China was seized by Chiang Kai-shek. His immediate policy was to unify China by (1) crushing the formidable opposition of the Chinese Communists who were militantly organized with armed forces in the field and (2) subjugating the various warlords, particularly those around the Peking area, each of whom had large personal armies. The military objectives of Chiang accentuated the chronic internal disorder of China and brought the threat of warfare to Manchuria, an area in which the Japanese had developed very extensive economic interests.

From 1924 to 1927 Baron Kijuro Shidehara, the Foreign Minister of Japan, tenaciously pursued a policy of friendly cooperation with China based on scrupulous adherence to the Washington treaties. Shidehara hoped to win the confidence and trust of both China and the United States in the motives and intentions of Japan in the Far East. However, his policy was from the beginning opposed by the militarists and nationalists who felt that it would only be interpreted as a sign of weakness and moreover would fail entirely in safeguarding the legitimate interests of Japan on the Asiatic mainland.

As the Kuomintang armies swept northward from Nanking and Shanghai to deal with the northern warlords, Japan dispatched troops into western Shantung to keep the war out of that province, in which she had important economic interests. This action antagonized the Chinese nationalists, but Chiang Kai-shek was then determined not be diverted from his immediate objective of unifying China and he by-passed the province so as to avoid incidents with Japanese forces.

In 1928 the Manchurian warlord, Chang Hsüeh-liang, unexpectedly proclaimed his allegiance to the Kuomintang Government. This action was of great concern to Japan because of her large economic interests in Manchuria and her policy of not regarding Manchuria as an integral part of China Proper. Relations between Japan and China rapidly deteriorated as the Kuomintang extended its political influence throughout Manchuria and began challenging Japan's interpretation of her treaty rights there.

By 1931 the militarists were in effective control of the government in Japan and prepared to carry out a positive policy in Manchuria, even in defiance of the Washington treaties, the Pact of Paris, and the Covenant of the League of Nations. By that time the militarists, ultranationalists and certain industrialists had come to regard Manchuria as of vital importance to the future of an industrial Japan that was poor in natural resources. Manchuria was believed to be an inexhaustible reservoir of coal, iron and other raw materials critically needed by the factories of Japan.

In 1931 a series of grave incidents occurred in Manchuria between Chinese and Japanese, culminating on September 18 in the blowing up of a small section of the South Manchuria Railroad. The Japanese promptly blamed the Chinese for the explosion ; and during the night of September 18 and 19, units of the Kwantung army moved swiftly and methodically, manifestly in accordance with a carefully prepared plan, and occupied the principal cities and strategic points of southern Manchuria. Chinese resistance was half-hearted and futile, and by the end of the year all of Manchuria was occupied. In February 1932 the Japanese established a puppet state, known as Manchukuo, and installed Henry

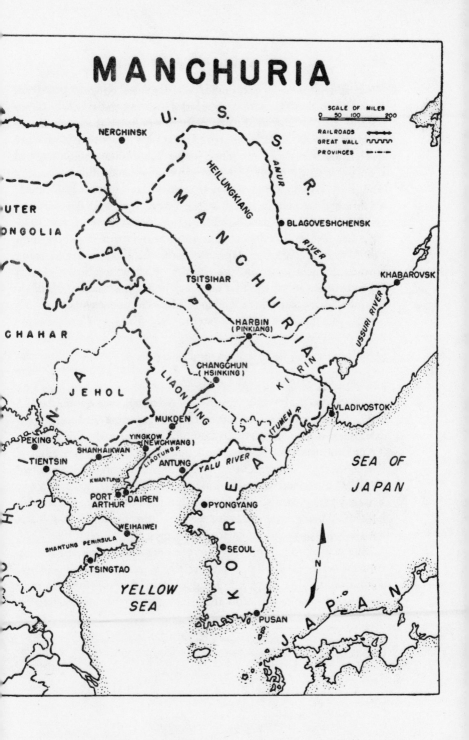

Pu-yi as regent.* In September the Japanese concluded a treaty with this new state, which assured Japan special rights in Manchukuo and authorized her to maintain military forces there.

Early in 1933 the Japanese troops resumed the offensive and conquered the province of Jehol. The Kuomintang Government then came to terms, and in May concluded the military Truce of Tangku. By the terms of this truce the Chinese were to evacuate a zone approximately south of the Great Wall and the Japanese were to have a free hand approximately north of the Great Wall. The Chinese were also to suppress anti-Japanese propaganda. On March 1, 1935 the Japanese took the final step and transformed the new state into the Empire of Manchukuo, with Henry Pu-yi proclaimed as the first emperor under the name of Kang-te. Though nominally independent, Manchukuo was now firmly within the Japanese empire system.

OPPOSITION OF THE UNITED STATES AND THE LEAGUE

Four days after the invasion of Manchuria, on September 22, 1931, Secretary Stimson informed the Japanese Ambassador in Washington that Japan was flagrantly violating the Nine-Power Treaty and the Pact of Paris and that it was the responsibility of the Japanese Government to bring its militarists under control. Stimson explained that he was aware of the sharp differences between Prime Minister Shidehara and the militarists.[1] Two days later the Japanese Ambassador assured Stimson that Japan " harbors no territorial designs in Manchuria."[2]

Meanwhile, the Chinese Government had appealed to the Council of the League of Nations, which immediately began consideration of the affair. A League resolution of September 30 recognized that a situation inimical to the peace existed in the

---

* Henry Pu-yi was the last " boy emperor " of China, who had been compelled to abdicate the Dragon Throne in 1912.

Far East and urged Japan to withdraw her troops and confine them to the railroad zone. Although not a member of the League, the United States from the outset of the Manchurian Affair cooperated with it to the fullest extent possible under the circumstances. When the League Council took up the Manchurian case in October, Prentis B. Gilbert, the American Minister in Switzerland, was authorized to sit in on the Council meetings as an unofficial observer on the invitation of the League. On October 24 the League invoked the Pact of Paris against Japan, but of course this action had not the slightest effect in restraining her. In December China and Japan both agreed to the League's proposal of a neutral commission of five members to make an on-the-spot investigation and report. This commission was headed by Lord Lytton and contained one American, General Frank R. McCoy.

While the Lytton Commission was busy with its investigation, Secretary Stimson, who continued to play an aggressive independent hand, although cooperating with the League as much as possible, on January 7, 1932 informed both Japan and China that the United States was confident the Lytton Commission would find an equitable solution to the Manchurian problem. More significantly, however, he warned both countries that the United States would not recognize any arrangement which impaired the treaty rights of the United States or violated the territorial integrity of China or the Open Door principle. He further warned that the United States would not recognize any changes brought about by the use of force in violation of the Pact of Paris.[3] In her evasive reply of January 16 Japan indicated that she intended to support the Open Door in China and to maintain it in both China Proper and Manchuria. Japan also stated that the Manchurian people would be permitted to establish their own government.[4] Although a Manchurian government was subsequently established, as indicated above, its creation had been manipulated by the Japanese and it was in effect under their control and domination.

Four days after Stimson reprimanded the Japanese, the British Foreign Office somewhat short-circuited him by making a public statement to the effect that Great Britain was confident Japan would respect the Open Door. It is to be noted that throughout the Manchurian crisis Great Britain played a passive role and failed to match or support the strong stand taken by Stimson, apparently because of the feeling that events in Manchuria were not of vital concern to her.

As the result of an assault on five Japanese subjects by a Chinese mob in Shanghai, Japan in January 1932 landed a force of seventy thousand troops there. To the surprise of the Japanese, these troops encountered heavy resistance in the fighting that ensued with Chinese troops, and they were given the first indication that while the Chinese had not resisted the Manchurian invasion with any serious effort they would do so where China Proper was concerned. Japanese retaliation resulted in the death of several thousand civilians, including women and children, which greatly angered the American public. The Japanese action was simply a retaliatory measure, however, and the troops were withdrawn shortly after their landing, thanks partly to the mediation efforts of the foreign diplomatic representatives in China.

Disappointed with the ineffectual action of the Council, China now pushed her case to the Assembly of the League of Nations. When that body met, the small powers presented a united front and exerted a considerable moral pressure on the big powers, all of whom seemed reluctant to take any positive action toward restraining Japan. On March 11 the Assembly adopted a resolution which proclaimed the Covenant of the League and the Pact of Paris binding on all concerned, and that the member states of the League would not recognize any treaty arrangement which violated either the Covenant or the Pact of Paris.[5] This latter statement was, manifestly, a reiteration of the Stimson Doctrine which had been announced more than two months before.

In October 1932 the Lytton Commission issued its report, based on its findings in Manchuria, and most of it was unfavorable to Japan. The report stated that the Japanese military operations of September 18–19 had not been in self-defense; that the Manchurian regime had not been established by the spontaneous will of the Manchurian people; and that the continuation of an independent Manchukuo was incompatible with the establishment of good relations between Japan and China. The report further advised that the restoration of the status quo ante would not be desirable. It instead recommended the establishment of an autonomous Manchuria as part of the Chinese Republic and the conclusion of a treaty between China and Japan which would recognize the latter's rights and interests in Manchuria.[6]

The League Assembly promptly endorsed the Lytton Report, and the State Department informed the League that the United States was in "substantial agreement" with its conclusions.[7] Yosuke Matsuoka and other members of the Japanese delegation then walked out of the League council room, never to return. Late in March 1933 Japan gave the required two-year notice of her intention to withdraw from the League, effective in 1935.

The League's actions during this major Far Eastern crisis were weak and ineffectual, to say the least, chiefly because none of the great powers considered their interests in Manchuria important enough to warrant the risk of war with Japan. The peace-seeking nations had yet to learn the hard lesson of the indivisibility of peace in this modern world. The League's most drastic action was to concur in the Stimson Doctrine of Non-Recognition; there was not even the faintest hint of the application of economic sanctions, let alone stronger measures. As for Secretary Stimson, he went further than the League and about as far as public opinion in the United States would permit, for at that time there was not one American in twenty who considered any Far Eastern issue worth the bone of a single American soldier.

With the excitement aroused by the Japanese occupation of Manchuria having subsided, it appeared for a short time in 1934 that the United States and Japan might find a formula for a modus vivendi concerning Manchukuo. In February of that year

Foreign Minister Koki Hirota informed Secretary Cordell Hull that: "I firmly believe that, viewed in the light of the broad aspects of the situation and studied from all possible angles, no question exists between our two countries that is fundamentally incapable of solution. I do not doubt that all issues pending between the two nations will be settled in a satisfactory manner, when examined with a good understanding on the part of each other's position, discussed with an open mind and in all frankness, and approached with a spirit of co-operation and conciliation."[8]

Two days after Kang-te was proclaimed Emperor of Manchukuo, Secretary Hull replied with an equally optimistic note, informing Hirota that he believed " there are in fact no questions between our two countries which, if they be viewed in proper perspective in both countries, can with any warrant be regarded as not readily susceptible to adjustment by pacific procedures."[9] But while Hirota's intentions at that time, as well as those of many other Japanese civilians, may have been sincere and motivated by a genuine desire to maintain friendly relations with the United States, the militarists were now in effective control and in a position to force policy and situations on the Foreign Minister and other civilian officials.

WIDENING OF THE JAPANESE-AMERICAN RIFT

The conciliatory attitude expressed by Hirota and Hull in February and March 1934 soon gave way to a widening of the rift between the United States and Japan. In violation of the Tangku Truce of 1933 the Japanese attempted to establish autonomous administrative councils in the provinces of northern China, in the hope of controlling them for the benefit of Japan and the furtherance of the long-range objective to dominate all China. While these efforts were not particularly successful, the Japanese nevertheless did succeed in flooding northern China with cheaply priced Japanese goods, largely in violation of existing Chinese tariff regulations.

Japan officially attributed her intervention in northern China to the disturbed internal situation prevailing in that area. On May 19, 1934 the Japanese Ambassador in Washington informed Hull that Japan had " a special interest in preserving peace and order in China." Hull countered with the observation that " many were wondering whether these claims or interests had ulterior or ultimate implications partaking of the nature of an over-lordship of the Orient."[10] On December 5, 1935, by which time there was ample evidence to indicate that the Japanese effort to establish autonomous councils in northern China was not meeting with any particular success, Hull in a press release announced that the developments in northern China were rightfully the concern of the United States as a treaty power.[11]

In 1934 Foreign Minister Hirota had laid down a three-point proposal as the sine qua non of Sino-Japanese friendship: (1) Sino-Japanese cooperation in combatting Communism, (2) Chinese recognition of the new state of Manchukuo, and (3) Chinese abandonment of the policy of playing off third powers against Japan. These proposals were naturally entirely unacceptable to China. They reflected the wishes, or even the demands, of the Kwantung army authorities who were then in complete control of Manchukuo and operating almost in total disregard of the civil government in Japan. Actually the Japanese Foreign Office was now reduced to the role of official apologist for the irresponsible actions of the Kwantung army, and usually on an ex post facto basis.

Meanwhile, the Japanese in Manchuria were working feverishly to transform that area into an arsenal of war. Hundreds of new factories were constructed, railroad lines were extended, and mines were intensively exploited. The aim, dictated by the Kwantung army, was to establish a Manchurian industry that would be capable of supplying a powerful army which would be permanently garrisoned in Manchukuo. To speed up this objective the economy of the region was regimented and centralized by the

Manchukuo Government, under the direction of the Japanese, and a number of measures were taken which seriously violated the Open Door principle. On November 14, 1934 the American Ambassador in Japan, Joseph Grew, informed Hull that while it was difficult to understand how the Japanese Government could ignore the pledges it had made to maintain the Open Door, it nevertheless "has done so."[12]

Grew made several specific protests to the Japanese Foreign Office concerning the violation of American rights in Manchuria. On November 30 he protested that a proposed oil monopoly in Manchuria adversely affected long established American interests, and he rejected the Japanese contention that this proposed monopoly was not within the knowledge or concern of the Japanese Government.[13]   In April of the following year (1935) Grew employed even stronger language, protesting that the monopoly would be a clear breach of treaty obligations.[14]   In December 1937 Grew also complained of the violation of American extraterritorial rights in Manchuria, and he protested to Hirota that these violations contravened existing treaties between the United States and China.[15]

The diplomatic exchanges between the United States and Japan concerning Manchuria were based on contradictory points of view in regard to its status.   The American position rested on the premise that Manchuria was still an integral part of China and that American rights there were still determined by the existing treaties with China.   Japan, on the other hand, contended that Manchukuo was an independent state and that American treaties with China had no validity in Manchukuo.   By 1937, however, the State Department, while still refusing to recognize Manchukuo, had practically reconciled itself to the Japanese fait accompli. Had the Japanese expansionists stopped with Manchukuo and had they been willing to negotiate in good faith on the issue of equal rights there, it is not altogether unlikely that de facto recognition of this state might not have come.

FURTHER WIDENING OF THE RIFT

After the conquest and assimilation of Manchuria, Japan boldly embarked on a new Asia policy which clearly violated both the spirit and the letter of the Washington treaties, the Covenant and the Pact of Paris. The outlines of this enlarged policy were made clear by a spokesman of the Japanese Foreign Office in April 1934 to the effect that Japan was opposed to China availing herself of the support of any third power to oppose Japan; that Japan was opposed to any power extending military or quasi-military assistance to China; and that Japan would not object to foreign assistance being extended to China of a non-military nature, financial or commercial, provided it did not in any way disturb the peace of the Far East. This policy was subsequently further expanded into what some Japanese euphemistically called the Monroe Doctrine for East Asia, based on the fundamental principle of Asia for the Asiatics with Japan as the custodial power.

Following the outbreak of the undeclared war against China in July 1937, the scope of Japanese expansionist policy was again extended. On July 7, 1939, two years after the outbreak of hostilities with China, the Japanese Ministers of War and the Navy were reported to have said that " all the people in the country must express their firm determination that Japan will never abandon her aim of making East Asia for East Asiatics." By 1940 Japan had clearly developed the idea of a Japan-Manchu-kuo-China bloc which was to function as a single " co-prosperity " economic unit. After the German occupation of the Netherlands and the defeat of France in the late spring of 1940, the co-prosperity idea was enlarged to include the regions of the southwestern Pacific. On June 29 of that year Foreign Minister Arita in a radio broadcast pointed out that the countries of East Asia and the regions of the southwestern Pacific were closely related to each other and destined to cooperate and supplement each other's economic needs as parts of a single economic sphere.[16] On August 1 Foreign Minister Matsuoka announced that Japan's aim was definitely to establish a Greater East Asia Co-Prosperity Sphere with the Japan-Manchukuo-China bloc as the core. By September 28 the Japanese Government had adopted a blueprint envisaging general peace with China and the establishment of a vast co-prosperity sphere embracing French Indochina, the Netherlands East Indies, the Straits Settlements, British Malaya, Thailand, the Philippines, British Borneo and Burma, with the Japan-Manchukuo-China bloc as the core.[17]

The doctrine of the Greater East Asia Co-Prosperity Sphere was intended primarily for Asiatic consumption outside Japan and was intended to appeal to the poverty-stricken peoples of Asia who were restive under the yoke of Western imperialism. Within Japan the doctrine that supplied the driving power and whipped up the fanaticism of the people was that of *Hakko Ichiu* (The World under One Roof). The roof of course was to be Japan, and sitting astride it was to be the Emperor.

THE SINO-JAPANESE UNDECLARED WAR

By the summer of 1937 it was clearly apparent that the restless Kwantung army was about to embark on new adventures at the expense of China. By this time the militarists and ultranationalists, and possibly most of the big industrialists, had come to believe that the resources of Manchuria were insufficient to support the vast industrial structure which Japan needed if she was to become the dominator of Asia. The extensive and largely undeveloped resources of China Proper came to be regarded as indispensable if Japan's greater aim was to be accomplished.

Although Chiang Kai-shek continued to feel that the Chinese Communists still represented a greater danger to China than the Japanese, he had by now come around to the position that if the Japanese invaded China Proper they would be resisted with all the force at his disposal and that even a temporary alliance with the Chinese Communists would be necessary. The Chinese Communists, on the other hand, had for a long time been advocating the expulsion of the Japanese from all of China. When war came with Japan, the Chinese Communists joined their military effort with that of the Kuomintang. Little did the United States, or even Chiang Kai-shek, realize at that time what bitter and earth-shaking developments were ultimately to come from this cooperation with the Communists. In going to war with Japan, Chiang Kai-shek lined up squarely with Kremlin policy, but history cruelly gave him no other alternatives.

The anticipated war came on July 7, 1937 when Japanese troops clashed with a contingent of Chinese troops in the vicinity of the ancient Marco Polo Bridge on the outskirts of Peking.* A temporary lull followed the skirmish, but on July 26 the Japanese launched a determined drive to clear the entire Peking-Tientsin area of all Chinese forces. On August 13 the Japanese carried the war to central China by landing troops in Shanghai and beginning a full-scale war against Chiang Kai-shek and the Kuomintang. The Japanese made no declaration of war: such a declaration would have been a violation of the Pact of Paris! The fundamental Japanese position, however, was that they were fighting Chiang Kai-shek and the usurping Kuomintang, not the Chinese people. Meanwhile, as has been indicated, Chiang Kai-shek had patched up a temporary truce with the Chinese Communists and, in theory at least, all China was now united to resist the Japanese aggressor.

Most Americans condemned the Japanese as lawless aggressors and sympathized with China, but only a small minority, although highly articulate, was willing to support the Government in taking a strong stand against Japan. Boycotts against Japanese goods were organized by private individuals and groups, but they had very little effect on the Japanese war effort, since regular trade continued. President Roosevelt refused to invoke the Neutrality

---

* This " incident " is commonly known as either the Marco Polo Bridge Incident or the Lukouchiao Incident.

Act of 1937* on the technical ground that since no declaration of war had been made the law was inapplicable. It was also believed by the Roosevelt administration that the invocation of the act would have benefited Japan and injured China since Japan was a highly developed industrial nation whereas China had very little industry and was highly dependent on imports of war equipment to sustain her military resistance. Actually the failure to invoke the act probably helped Japan as much as, if not more than, it helped China, for it enabled her to acquire from the United States huge quantities of scrap and oil and other raw materials critically needed by her war industries.

During the early phase of the Sino-Japanese war the State Department exerted considerable effort to bring about a cessation of hostilities. On July 21, two weeks after the outbreak of the Marco Polo Bridge Incident, Secretary Hull informed Japan that the United States was anxious to bring about peace between China and Japan and that it would be glad to do anything short of mediation toward composing the differences between China and Japan.[18] On August 10, about two weeks after the Japanese launched their drive to clear the Peking-Tientsin area, the United States made an outright offer of its good offices for the settlement of the controversy,[19] which was politely but firmly rejected by Japan. Ten days after the Japanese had landed troops in Shanghai for their big drive, the State Department urged both belligerents to refrain from further hostilities and reiterated the determination of the United States to regard all pertinent treaties as in force, particularly the Washington treaties and the Pact of Paris.[20] Several protests were also made to Japan concerning the aerial bombing of non-combatants.

By the end of September 1937 the attitude of the Roosevelt

---

* The Neutrality Act of 1937 provided that when the President recognized the existence of a state of war between belligerents, restrictions would be placed on loans and the export of munitions. Goods authorized for export would have to be picked up by the buyer: this was known as the " cash and carry " provision.

administration toward Japan had greatly hardened. This hardening attitude was reflected in instructions given the American Minister in Switzerland to the effect that whereas China from the beginning had agreed to conciliation, Japan had been opposed to consultations with any third powers and on the contrary had expanded her military operations in China. The Minister was also informed that the issues had gone far beyond violations of particular treaties and now involved questions of international law, principles of humanity, war and peace.[21]

Protests against the alleged inhuman conduct of the war by Japan were made by both the League and the United States. With the Japanese extension of the theater of war, it was inevitable that some Americans would get hurt. As early as September 17 Grew had protested to Hirota concerning "attacks by Japanese armed forces in China upon American nationals and their property, including attacks upon American humanitarian and philanthropic establishments and upon persons and property of non-combatants generally."[22] Five days later Grew made a second protest against Japanese actions which he alleged were jeopardizing American lives, and he rejected the Japanese proposal that Americans should evacuate Nanking (which was then under attack).[23] On September 27 the League of Nations Advisory Committee vigorously protested the Japanese bombing of what it called open cities and expressed "profound distress at the loss of life caused to innocent civilians, including great numbers of women and children."[24] A State Department press release of the following day reasserted that Japanese bombings violated the principles of law and humanity.[24] On October 6 the League of Nations Assembly condemned the Japanese actions in China as "out of all proportion to the incident that occasioned the conflict." The Assembly further contended that "no justification can be found either on the basis of legal instruments or the right of self-defense" for the Japanese operations which were in violation of the Nine-Power Treaty and the Pact of Paris.[25] On the same day the State Department supported this position.

As the Japanese pressed their drives with startling initial success and their hope of quickly bringing Chiang Kai-shek to terms seemed probable, President Roosevelt became intensely hostile to Japan. In a speech at Chicago early in October 1937 he tested the extent to which American public opinion would support a really strong policy against Japan. This was the famous " quarantine speech " which vaguely suggested the quarantining of aggressor nations that contributed to the growing " international anarchy." " Surely," he said, " the 90 percent who want to live in peace under law in accordance with moral standards that have received almost universal acceptance through the centuries, can and must find some way to make their will prevail." He hinted that the Administration was prepared to take a firm stand against Japan with the words: " There must be positive endeavors to preserve the peace."[27] The speech was hailed by the internationalists the world over, but in the United States popular reaction was so unfavorable that the President felt compelled to beat something of a hasty retreat from the position he had publicly taken far in advance of public opinion. Needless to say, the public's disapproval of this speech was based on its unwillingness to become involved in actions that might lead to an overseas war rather than disagreement with the President's severe indictment of Japan and other so-called aggressor nations.

In November 1937 the United States and eighteen other nations participated in a conference at Brussels for the purpose of " studying the amicable means of hastening the end of the unfortunate conflict." The conference was called in accordance with a provision of the Nine-Power Treaty of 1922. Japan declined the invitation to attend the conference on the ground that the League had already " taken the part of China against Japan."[28] Germany also declined an invitation to participate, and Italy, although participating, opposed coercive measures and termed them " irresponsible." The American delegate, Norman H. Davis, was instructed to take what action he could to preserve peace but at the same time to do what was possible to check the Japanese aggression. The conference, which convened from November 3 to 24, took no stronger action than to condemn Japan and to accuse the Japanese " of having decided in substance that it is Japan's objective to destroy the will and the ability of China to resist the will and demands of Japan."[29]

On December 12, 1937 a serious crisis arose as a result of Japanese planes deliberately bombing and sinking the U.S. gunboat *Panay* and three ships of the Standard Oil Company which were being used to evacuate American citizens from the war zones. Foreign Minister Hirota immediately apologized to Ambassador Grew and explained that the Japanese aviators because of poor visibility had mistaken the American ships for Chinese vessels transporting fleeing Chinese troops.* He pledged that Japan would make prompt indemnification. A State Department note, written the day before Hirota made his explanations, termed the bombing a violation of American rights and demanded an expression of regret and complete indemnification.[30] The Japanese Government was prepared to offer full satisfaction, and in April 1938 paid the full amount claimed by the United States with a check for $2,214,000. This closed the incident.

Meanwhile, the State Department undertook the evacuation of all American citizens from the war zones and made ships available for that purpose. Early in 1938 American marines were evacuated from Shanghai and infantry troops were withdrawn from Tientsin. The former troops had been dispatched to Shanghai during the *Panay* crisis, while the latter had been stationed in the Tientsin area in accordance with provisions of the Boxer Protocol of 1900.

Despite the evacuation of American citizens, the State Department made it clear that it had no intention of abandoning American treaty rights as expressed in the treaties with China which it still considered binding. Between January and April 1938 Grew made four protests to Hirota concerning violations of Chinese

---

* Subsequent evidence disclosed that it was a clear day. Apparently the Japanese aviators had been poorly informed concerning their bombing targets.

tariffs by the North China provisional regime, which had been established under Japanese auspices, and also concerning the occupation, looting and destruction of American properties in several parts of China.

In October Grew made a spirited defense of American treaty rights, protesting that the Open Door was being flagrantly violated and that unwarranted restrictions were being imposed on American citizens remaining in areas of China under Japanese control. "Equality of opportunity or the Open Door has virtually ceased to exist in Manchuria," he said, "notwithstanding the assurances of the Japanese Government that it would be maintained in that area."[31] These charges had been repeatedly made by the United States Government and Grew apparently made them for the record rather than in any naïve hope that they might at this late date alter the policies to which the militarists had committed Japan.

In its reply of November 18 the Japanese Government made it clear that a "new situation" had developed in the Far East which made the treaties supporting the old concept of the Open Door obsolete. The Japanese note contended that it would be "useless to attempt to reconcile the principle of the open door, as understood in the United States and elsewhere abroad, with the new situation which Japan was endeavoring to bring about." "As long as these points are understood," explained the note, "Japan has not the slightest inclination to oppose the participation of the United States and other powers in the great work of reconstructing Asia along lines of industry and trade."[32] In its reply to this note the State Department categorically refused to recognize any "new order" and further suggested that if Japan were dissatisfied with the provisions of the old treaties governing the rights and privileges of foreign nations in China she should take steps to negotiate new ones.[33]

This exchange of notes revealed that as far as Japan was concerned the old concept of the Open Door and all the treaties based on its premises were dead because of the "new order" and the "new situation" she was establishing in East Asia. It was equally clear that Japan had no intention of prohibiting American capital and commercial interests from participating in the development of China, but it was to be on Japan's terms rather than on the basis of the old treaties. Since the United States was firmly committed not to recognize any changes brought about by the use of force or any unilateral denunciation of treaties, it was now apparent that a serious and seemingly irreparable rift had developed between the United States and Japan.

EFFECT OF THE WAR IN EUROPE

By 1939 Japan appeared to be mired in the China war. Although huge areas of China were under Japanese occupation, there still remained large areas to be conquered and held. Even in the occupied areas, actual Japanese control was restricted to cities, railroads and communication lines. The Chinese had somewhat recovered from the initial disasters and were offering stiff resistance, while American moral support helped to brace Chinese morale. There were no indications of a Chinese military collapse or of a desire for peace on Japan's terms. It was evident that a long and bitter struggle lay ahead before the Japanese could achieve their objectives.

In June 1939 the Japanese launched an intensive drive to weaken Western influence in China which elicited from Secretary Hull a warning that the United States would definitely not recognize any "new order" established by the unilateral action of Japan in the Far East. On July 26 the State Department took one of its strongest actions up to that time when it denounced the Commercial Treaty of 1911, which was scheduled to expire on January 26 of the following year. This was not a treaty violation, for a clause of the treaty permitted its denunciation with a six-months' notice. This action gravely concerned Japan, for the war effort against China was highly dependent on certain materials being received from the United States as well as from Southeast

Asia and the southwestern Pacific area. Although no new treaty was negotiated when it expired in 1940, the effects on Japan were not critically serious. Trade with Japan continued on a treaty-less basis, for Roosevelt was reluctant to impose an embargo on trade with Japan because of the fear that the Japanese militarists might be driven to invade the Netherlands East Indies, which were an important source of vitally needed raw materials. There had been some curtailment of shipments to Japan, however, and as early as 1938 the State Department had requested manufacturers not to export planes since they were being used to bomb help-less civilians.

The outbreak of the war in Europe in September 1939 involving Great Britain and Germany in a titanic struggle greatly encouraged the Japanese militarists. But for their fear of Russia, which was then neutral and only ostensibly allied with Germany, they might have plunged into an all-out effort to crush China with all the forces at their disposal. The increasingly hostile attitude of the Roose-velt administration also served as a deterrent on the Japanese militarists. Consequently only a part of the Japanese military potential was being employed against China; the remainder was being held in reserve, and augmented, for possible contingencies. It was recognized by the Japanese that with war raging in Europe, only the United States stood between them and the achievement of their objectives in China. Nevertheless, the Japanese Govern-ment at this time was intent on a policy of not becoming involved in a war with the United States.

On April 15, 1940, when it appeared that a German invasion of the Netherlands was imminent, Japan expressed deep concern about the future of the oil-and-rubber-rich Netherlands East Indies.[34] Two days later Hull made it clear that the United States was also vitally concerned about any changes that might be brought about in the East Indies by force, and he reminded Japan of her obligations under the Root-Takahira Agreement of 1908 and the Four-Power Treaty of 1922.[35]

In July, following the successful German invasion and occupation of the Netherlands, the Japanese Government was reorganized with Prince Fumimaro Konoe installed as Prime Minister and Yosuke Matsuoka as Foreign Minister. This cabinet reorganization signified that a stronger policy would be adopted against the United States and that closer orientation would be effected with Germany and Italy. The change in government also held ominous forebodings of redoubled efforts to crush China and of possible moves in the direction of the Netherlands Indies.

The United States countered by intensifying its economic warfare against Japan. The Roosevelt administration apparently believed, for a time, that the tightening of economic restrictions against Japan and the drying up of sources of oil, rubber and other strategic materials might adversely affect the Japanese war industries and serve as a deterrent on the militarists. At any rate, the export of all munitions and products used in their manufacture was prohibited unless specifically licensed by the State Department. The same restriction was also placed on the export of oil and scrap iron. This action was squarely directed against Japan and was highly encouraging to the embattled Chinese who had never been able to comprehend the Administration's policy of strongly condemning Japan and at the same time continuing to supply her with critically needed war materials.

After the surrender of the French forces in June to the invading German armies and the establishment of a collaborationist regime in Vichy, it was feared that the Japanese would take advantage of this situation to gain a strategic foothold in French Indochina. These fears came to pass in September when the Konoe Government extorted concessions for strategic bases in northern Indochina from the helpless representatives of the Vichy Government in Indochina.* With these bases the Japanese hoped to choke off the flow of supplies into China along the Indochina border.

---

* The Vichy Government was headed by Marshal Pétain and Pierre Laval. It administered that part of France unoccupied by the Germans, and throughout the war collaborated with Germany. The French officials in Indochina remained loyal to it.

Strong protests were made by Grew and Hull, and the United States Government also countered with a loan of $25,000,000 to China. Following the Japanese occupation of these bases, the State Department made several protests concerning violations of American property rights there.

Late in September Germany, Italy and Japan concluded a tripartite military pact which was clearly directed against the United States. It provided for a common military effort in case any of the three signatory powers were attacked by a neutral power. As Hull stated, this pact did not substantially alter a situation that had already existed for some time. The announcement of the pact failed to intimidate the Administration, and it countered shortly after with a proposal to the Congress for the establishment of a lend-lease program to assist all nations fighting the Axis powers and their allies.

THE DRIFT TOWARD WAR

In November Japan concluded a treaty with the puppet government of Wang Ching-wei that had been established in Japanese-occupied China under the auspices of the Japanese. This treaty provided for Sino-Japanese cooperation and the withdrawal of Japanese troops from China two years after the termination of the war against the Chiang Kai-shek regime. The Japanese establishment of this puppet regime was a clear indication that they had abandoned all hope of ever bringing Chiang Kai-shek to terms by negotiation and that they were consequently resolved to destroy his regime by force of arms.

The Wang Ching-wei Government had been established in March, but it had never been recognized by the State Department. On the day following the conclusion of the Japanese treaty with Wang Ching-wei, Roosevelt retaliated by proclaiming that the United States intended to lend China an additional $100,000,000. Two days later the Treasury Department advanced China $50,000,-000 for the stabilization of her currency. Roosevelt therefore had made it clear that, as far as his powers would permit it, he would not abandon China.

Early in 1941 Japan renewed her efforts to arrive at an understanding with the United States. A new Japanese ambassador, Kichisaburo Nomura, was received by President Roosevelt on February 14, and several conferences were subsequently held by the Ambassador with Secretary Hull. Very little headway was made, however, because of the Japanese position that the United States should cease backing Chiang Kai-shek and because of Japan's firm adherence to the Tripartite Pact with Germany and Italy.* The impossibility of an agreement became apparent on May 12 when Nomura proposed a general settlement between the United States and Japan on the basis of the so-called " Konoe principles " which had been incorporated in the treaty between Japan and the Wang Ching-wei puppet regime. Further clarification by Nomura disclosed that acquiescence to these " principles " would have given Japan a special position in China and extensive economic rights in the southwestern Pacific such as Japan herself was totally unwilling to allow any third power in China.[36] Consequently, the discussions bogged down and an impasse had seemingly been reached.

Foreign Minister Matsuoka had visited Berlin and Rome early in the year to strengthen the ties with the Axis. On his return to Japan via Russia he stopped in Moscow and concluded a non-aggression pact with the Soviet Union. The pact was signed on April 13. It provided that each signatory would respect the territorial integrity of the other's possessions and that in case either party were attacked by a third power the other would remain neutral. The pact was to remain in force for five years. A joint Russo-Japanese declaration was also issued in which Japan pledged to respect the territorial integrity of the People's

---

* The Roosevelt administration by this time had committed itself to a policy of " all-out " assistance to Great Britain with all means short of actual armed assistance. It had made it clear that the United States would not permit the Axis powers to beat Great Britain.

Republic of Mongolia, a Soviet puppet state, and Russia pledged to respect the territorial integrity of Manchukuo.

The pact was a blow to Chiang Kai-shek, particularly since China already had a non-aggression pact with Russia. Needless to say, the pact freed Japan from anxiety concerning the Manchurian frontier with Siberia and enabled her to concentrate on a drive into Southeast Asia and the East Indies. Just as the Molotov-Ribbentrop Pact of August 1939* had given Germany the green light for the invasion of Poland, so did this pact pave the way for a bold Japanese move into the southwestern Pacific area.

Japan's decision to drive southward for the necessary resources of the southwestern Pacific area was not substantially altered by the unexpected German invasion of Russia in late June, although for a very brief period this sudden development did throw the Japanese Government into something of a quandary. The tremendous power of the German assault required Russia to marshal the bulk of her military strength in Europe to resist Germany and left her Far Eastern garrisons too weak for any possible offensive action against Japan.

At an imperial conference summoned on July 2 by General Hideki Tojo, it was agreed to launch a drive into the southwestern Pacific area and to prepare for possible war against the United States and Great Britain. The first step in this drive would be to bring all French Indochina under Japanese control. It was also agreed to make discreet preparations against Russia and to invade Siberia in case the defeat of Russia became imminent.[37] In that month, and again in September, the Japanese fleet carried out secret maneuvers based on a plan drawn up by Admiral Yamamoto, which was eventually used in the attack on Pearl Harbor.[38]

---

* This was a non-aggression pact between Germany and Russia, concluded on August 22. It freed Germany from anxiety concerning her frontier with Russia and enabled her to invade Poland and risk the intervention of Great Britain and France.

Late in July the Japanese revealed their intentions when by duress they obtained additional bases in southern Indochina. This action greatly worsened the already severely strained relations between the United States and Japan. The State Department promptly announced that these bases were obtained " primarily for the purpose of further and more obvious movements of conquest in adjacent areas."[39] On July 25, two days after the French officials in Indochina had granted the bases, the State Department took one of its most drastic actions by freezing all Japanese assets in the United States. Japan immediately countered with similar measures. Economic relations between the United States and Japan now became virtually paralyzed.

THE FAILURE OF DIPLOMACY

During August and September relations improved slightly between the United States and Japan as a result of renewed and strenuous efforts on the part of Japan to arrive at a modus vivendi with the United States. Hopes for a rapprochement of some kind reached their high point on August 28 when Prince Konoe, the Japanese Prime Minister, stressed the peaceful intentions of Japan and urged President Roosevelt to meet with him for a personal discussion of the existing differences. Roosevelt replied by suggesting that preliminary discussions between officials of the two governments should precede such a meeting, but nothing tangible resulted.

The position of the Japanese militarists then stiffened, and this was reflected in proposals presented on September 6 by Ambassador Nomura which were much less conciliatory than those embodied in his previous discussions.[40] On the day that Nomura presented these proposals, a second imperial conference was held in Tokyo at which it was agreed to complete military preparations by the end of October for possible war against the United States, Great Britain and the Netherlands. It was also decided at this conference that a last effort would be made to obtain Japan's demands by diplomatic means, but should diplomacy fail war would be begun late in October.[41]

On October 16 the Konoe Government fell, and on the following day a new government was organized by General Tojo. The new government was an out-and-out military government, and was determined either to reach an immediate diplomatic settlement substantially on Japan's terms or to break the paralyzing effects of the economic blockade by overt military action in Southeast Asia and the East Indies.

As a last diplomatic resort, the crack trouble shooter Saburo Kurusu was flown to Washington to assist Nomura in the delicate and almost hopeless task of reconciling Japanese-American differences. Tojo apparently believed there was a "thirty percent" chance of peace being preserved, primarily because the United States was insufficiently prepared for war and most Americans were opposed to involvement in hostilities in the Far East. Tojo insisted that Japan would under no circumstances agree to withdrawal from China. Kurusu was instructed to complete his discussions no later than the end of November, and in the meantime the Tojo Government stepped up its preparations for the eventuality of war with the United States.[42] On his arrival in San Francisco, Kurusu admitted that there didn't appear to be much hope for an agreement but he "hoped to go through the line for a touchdown."

At a third imperial conference in Tokyo on November 5 the Japanese leaders in control of the government agreed that war would be begun shortly with the United States, in which case the following would be accomplished: (1) an agreement would be concluded with Germany and Italy not to make a separate peace; (2) the independence of the Philippines would be proclaimed at the earliest possible moment; (3) independence would be granted to Burma and.to part of the Dutch East Indies; (4) support would be given to the independence movement in India; and (5) Thailand would be supported in her effort to recover territories lost to Great Britain in the past.[43] Manifestly, these intentions were for the purpose of transforming the forthcoming war into a great crusade for the liberation of the Asiatic peoples from the yoke of Western imperialism.

Military movements of the Japanese during the next few days made it apparent to the whole world that Japan was about to strike somewhere with her armed might. The wily Churchill, Britain's wartime Prime Minister, was fully aware of the highly explosive situation in the Far East, and in a speech of November 10 he announced that " should the United States be involved in war with Japan, a British declaration will follow within an hour."[44] Four days later Nomura remonstrated to his Government that its position and attitude would lead to war with the United States.

On November 20 Nomura and Kurusu presented to Secretary Hull the last proposals of the Japanese Government. Japan would desist from further advances in Southeast Asia and the East Indies on condition that the United States would resume full commercial intercourse and that the shipment of needed materials from the Netherlands East Indies would also be resumed.* In addition, the United States was to cease all assistance to China.[45] These proposals were, of course, totally unacceptable to the State Department. Acceptance of these terms would have been a betrayal of China, condonement of past Japanese aggressions, encouragement of future aggressions, and total abandonment of traditional American Far Eastern policy.[46]

On November 26 the State Department presented a note to Kurusu and Nomura which proved to be the last offer to the Japanese Government. The note contained both general and specific proposals. The general proposals suggested an agreement on basic principles which were traditional American Far Eastern policy, the abolition of excessive restrictions on trade, and equal access to sources of raw materials. The specific proposals suggested: (1) the conclusion of a non-aggression pact among

---

* Following the lead of the United States and Great Britain, the Netherlands Government in Exile, which still retained control over the East Indies, had also suspended commercial relations with Japan.

Japan, the United States, the British Empire, Soviet Russia, Thailand, and the Netherlands; (2) recognition by Japan of the government of Chiang Kai-shek as the exclusive government of all China; (3) the surrender of extraterritorial rights in China by the United States and Japan; (4) the withdrawal of all Japanese military, naval, air and police forces from China and Indochina; and (5) the conclusion of a new commercial treaty in which the United States would place raw silk on the free list.[47]

It is hard to believe that the State Department had the slightest hope that the Japanese Government, firmly controlled by the militarists, would accept any substantial part of the proposals, let alone all of them. It was as impossible for the Japanese Government to accept these terms as it was for the State Department to accept the Japanese proposals of November 20. Japanese acceptance of the terms would have been a betrayal of the Axis, abandonment of the Wang Ching-wei Government which it had established, and a renunciation of Japan's dreams of a privileged position in the Far East because of her geographical position, her political primacy and her economic superiority. To accept the demands in toto the militarists would have had to repudiate themselves and tacitly confess to the Japanese people and the world at large that their actions had been unlawful and evil. Governments never make such a confession unless forced to do so by circumstances beyond their control.

On the day the United States presented its last proposals, Nomura and Kurusu cabled Tokyo that the negotiations could now be considered a failure.[48] For its part, the Tojo Government regarded further diplomatic discussions as futile, and prepared for bold and decisive action. The Pearl Harbor attacking fleet was assembled at Tankan Bay* for the fateful attack,[49] and it was decided to keep up the appearance of further negotiations as a screen until the hour arrived for the actual beginning of the attack.

---

* Tankan is a bay of Etorofu, the largest island of the Kurile group.

Three days after the delivery of the November 26 note, Secretary Hull confided to the British Ambassador that " the diplomatic part of our relations with Japan was virtually over and that the matter will now go to officials of the Army and Navy." He further confided that a sudden Japanese military move was possible at any time. Known Japanese troop movements clearly indicated, in fact, that the Tojo Government was liable to go to war at any moment. As though completely aware of the lateness of the hour, Roosevelt on December 6 telegraphed a personal message to the Emperor of Japan in which he appealed for joint endeavors to avert the " tragic responsibilities " of war. Both he and the Emperor, he stated, had " a sacred duty to restore traditional amity and prevent further death and destruction in the world."[50] Unfortunately, this message did not reach the hands of the Emperor until after actual hostilities had broken out between Japan and the United States. Even had the message been delivered promptly, it is very unlikely that anything could have been done by the Emperor at that late hour to avoid the catastrophe, since neither Japan nor the United States was willing to retreat from its fixed position and meet the other on middle ground.

At the fourth imperial conference of December 1 the final decision was made to declare war against the United States, Great Britain and the Netherlands.[51] The Japanese Foreign Minister, Shigenori Togo, then instructed Nomura to deliver the final Japanese reply " at 1300 on the 7th your time."[52] It was actually at 1420 hours on December 7, Washington time, that Nomura handed the official reply of the Japanese Government to Secretary Hull. The American proposals were categorically rejected. Both the United States and Great Britain were accused of obstructing Japan's efforts to establish peace in East Asia and of seeking to maintain and strengthen their dominant position in China and other areas of East Asia. The note concluded with the ominous words that it was " impossible to reach an agreement through further negotiation."[53]

Meanwhile, the dreaded conflict had already broken out. More than an hour before Nomura handed the note to Hull, the Japanese forces had begun the surprise attack on the American fleet at Pearl Harbor. It was Ambassador Grew in Tokyo who was first informed of the outbreak of hostilities. Needless to say, the Pearl Harbor attack was one of the greatest military disasters in American history. Five battleships, three destroyers and a target vessel were sunk, more than four hundred planes were destroyed, and 2,117 persons were killed. In addition, three battleships and many other ships were damaged and serious destruction was wrought on installations. The success of the Japanese attack was far greater than anything they had anticipated, and chiefly because the defenders were caught napping and unprepared.

For two years the American public had been bitterly divided on foreign policy and the issue of intervention in Europe and the Far East. What Roosevelt and his administration had been unable to accomplish toward gaining united American support was accomplished by the Japanese planes in a few brief moments when they hurled death and destruction at Pearl Harbor. Almost instantly the American people buried their differences and united to defend the " sacred honor " of the country and to avenge Pearl Harbor. The morning after the attack, the Congress immediately acted on the President's request for a declaration of war against Japan. There was only one dissenting vote in both Houses.

Two days after Pearl Harbor, President Roosevelt warned the nation that Germany and Italy regarded as enemies all nations which were not on the side of the Axis powers. Although they had not formally declared war against the United States, said the President, they " consider themselves at war with the United States at this moment as much as they consider themselves at war with Britain and Russia. It would serve us ill to merely eliminate Japan and find the rest of the world dominated by Hitler and Mussolini."[54]

Was the President preparing to ask the Congress for a declaration of war against Germany and Italy also? At any rate, the two

Axis nations themselves proclaimed a state of war two days later. On that same day, without a single dissenting vote, both Houses of the Congress declared war on Germany and Italy, and hence the war in the West and the war in the East merged into " one war " of unprecedented magnitude and frightfulness.

CHAPTER VII

THE GREAT PACIFIC WAR

STEMMING THE AXIS AVALANCHE

On New Year's day, 1942, twenty-six allied nations at war with the Axis powers formally united in a military alliance, known as the United Nations, which was to be the nucleus of the later United Nations peace organization.* In an impressive formal declaration to the world, each of the subscribing nations pledged adherence to the high principles of the Atlantic Charter and vowed not to make a separate peace with any of the Axis powers. The Atlantic Charter had been promulgated by Roosevelt and Churchill in August 1941, when the United States was still non-belligerent although no longer neutral in the wars raging in Europe and in Asia. It enunciated the principles on which they would base their hopes for a better world, and it specifically denounced territorial aggrandizement or any territorial changes which did not " accord with the freely expressed wishes of the people concerned." Needless to say, this provision was cruelly violated by the Allied powers in the settlements which they imposed on Germany, Italy and Japan.

---

* Nations signing the initial United Nations agreement were: the United States, Great Britain, the Soviet Union, China; and Australia, Belgium, Canada, Costa Rica, Cuba, Czechoslovakia, the Dominican Republic, El Salvador, Greece, Guatemala, Haiti, Honduras, India, Luxemburg, the Netherlands, New Zealand, Nicaragua, Norway, Panama, Poland, South Africa and Yugoslavia. During the course of the war nineteen other nations signed the agreement.

The entrance of the United States in the great holocaust did not immediately slow down the military successes of the Axis powers. At least until the latter half of 1942 it almost seemed as though the Axis nations could not be beaten. In the European theater the Germans and their allies continued to roll forward. In the Pacific area the Japanese won a rapid series of brilliant victories. The Philippines and Hongkong fell easily. The great British base at Singapore, which had been believed to be almost impregnable, was captured by means of an unanticipated assault through the jungles of Malaya, brilliantly executed by General Yamashita. The vast Netherlands East Indies, with their critically needed resources of oil and rubber, were conquered and occupied piecemeal. A vast number of islands scattered throughout the enormous expanses of the Pacific were also occupied. With the U.S. fleet badly crippled as a result of the devastating Pearl Harbor attack, the American forces under the supreme command of General MacArthur could do nothing more than wage dogged retreating tactics. By June 1942 the Japanese had achieved the peak of their success in the Pacific War. An enormous farflung empire with fabulous resources had been brought under Japanese occupation and control. Japanese forces poised in Burma threatened to drive into India and perhaps link up with German forces who might conceivably begin a drive through the Near and Middle East. American military power had been thrust eastward and southward many thousands of miles from the Japanese home islands.

The Japanese high command apparently believed that Japan could now fall back on the defensive and hold America at bay along the great perimeter of the Japanese conquests. They also apparently believed that Japan could continue a defensive war indefinitely and that the United States would eventually tire of the futile struggle and agree to a negotiated peace which would leave Japan in possession of many of her gains. The high command miscalculated, however, on at least two major assumptions: (1) that Japan would have sufficient time and the ability to exploit

adequately the critically needed resources of the conquered regions; and (2) that the United States could not mount sufficient air and naval power to overcome the disadvantages of long supply lines and the lack of adequate advance bases. They also failed to anticipate that American submarines would turn the entire western Pacific into a sea of destruction for Japanese warships and merchantmen. During the course of the war American submarines sent millions of tons of Japanese shipping to the bottom of the sea. These staggering losses gradually made it impossible for Japan to furnish adequate logistical support to its widely scattered troops. Toward the close of the war the shipping losses also crippled the Japanese home island production of war materials because of the deprivation of critically needed supplies of raw materials from the Pacific and continental areas.

The latter part of 1942 was the turning point of the great war, in Europe as well as in the Pacific area. The war in the Pacific was, of course, an integral part of the war in Europe, for World War II was in every respect a global war. Successes or reverses in one theater were bound to have an effect on the other theater. The German armies reached the pinnacle of their success in December 1942 when they threatened the three critically important Russian defensive centers of Leningrad, Moscow and Stalingrad. The Germans failed to capture any of these three bitterly contested points, and in 1943 were forced to begin a disastrous withdrawal. From then on, German military power declined precipitately. In the Mediterranean area the Axis powers also began decisive retreats. North Africa was completely overrun by the Allied forces, and in July Sicily was invaded. On September 9 Italy accepted unconditional surrender terms. Although Mussolini continued the struggle in northern Italy as the head of a shoddy Fascist Republic, this was the first serious break in the Axis front and marked the accelerated decline of Axis fortunes.

Meanwhile, in the Pacific area the Allied military forces under the command of General MacArthur and the Allied naval forces under the command of Admiral Nimitz, carrying out " grandiose

strategy," rapidly turned the fortunes of war and began driving
the Japanese back toward their home islands. The initial tide of
Japanese military successes had been halted in the great naval
Battle of Midway early in June 1942. In that battle American
fleets under the command of Admirals Raymond A. Spruance and
Frank J. Fletcher inflicted heavy losses on the Japanese fleet.
With this victory the safety of Hawaii was assured, and the turning point in the Pacific War had been reached. Two months
later American marines under General Alexander A. Vandergrift
gained a foothold on the island of Guadalcanal. The savage fight
for this island lasted six months, but by February 1943 the entire
island was securely in American hands. This victory assured
the safety of Australia. By mid-August 1943 the Japanese were
driven out of the Aleutian Islands, and in November American
forces landed on the island of Tarawa. The initiative had now
definitely passed to America.

By the end of 1943 the Axis powers were facing inevitable
defeat in both Europe and the Pacific area. In both theaters the
definitive defeat was merely a matter of time. Despite the in-
evitability of defeat, both Germany and Japan continued the
struggle valiantly. Sober minds in both countries knew that
continuation of the war was hopeless, but in both countries the
dictatorial power of the government was so absolute that no men
or groups were able to make their will felt. Furthermore, neither
the United States nor its allies appeared willing to offer a peace
on " reasonably honorable " terms which the dissidents in Germany and Japan could accept and demand without fear of being
damned as traitors. By the end of 1943 the United Nations had
made it painfully clear to the Axis powers that peace could be
obtained only on the basis of unconditional surrender.

CAIRO AND TEHERAN

During World War II the United States for the first time in its
history became formally associated with other warring nations as

an " allied " power. For the first time, also, the President on numerous occasions departed from the territorial limits of the United States to participate personally in several conferences. Most of the wartime " diplomacy " with the so-called allies was, of course, of a secret nature, and the agreements concluded were executive understandings made by the President without consulting or obtaining the approval of the Congress. Of the principal wartime conferences, four had an important bearing on the Far East and Japan, namely: Cairo, Teheran, Yalta and Potsdam.

At the Cairo Conference President Roosevelt conferred with Winston Churchill and Chiang Kai-shek on problems of the Pacific War. Since Soviet Russia was not then at war with Japan, and was in fact committed to a non-aggression pact with her, Russian representatives did not participate in the Cairo discussions. Roosevelt was accompanied by a number of high-ranking officials, including General Eisenhower, Admiral Leahy, Admiral McIntire and Harry Hopkins. Discussions among Roosevelt, Churchill and Chiang Kai-shek began on November 22 and lasted four days.

An official communique was issued on December first which announced to the world that the United States, Great Britain and China had agreed that Japan was to be restrained and punished for her crimes; that she was to be stripped of all lands seized or occupied since the beginning of World War I in 1914; that all territories taken from China were to be returned, such as Manchuria, Formosa and the Pescadores Islands; and that Korea was to become free and independent. In other words, not only was Japan to be punished but she was also to be deprived of her entire Empire and restricted to her confined island possessions prior to 1895.

From Cairo Roosevelt flew to Teheran for a personal meeting with Premier Stalin. Whereas Churchill and his staff were housed in the British embassy, Roosevelt and his staff were quartered in the Russian embassy, on the insistence of the Russians, who felt that the President could be better protected there from the machinations of the Nazi agents who were operating in Iran. At Teheran Roosevelt at long last met Stalin personally, something he had been trying to accomplish almost since the United States entered the war.

Roosevelt acted as presiding officer of the joint discussions which followed. He outlined to Stalin the tremendously far-flung military operations then in progress against Japan which involved more than a million men. Stalin expressed his appreciation of this American effort and promised that after Germany was defeated and sufficient Russian military strength had been transported to the Far East, the Soviet Union would enter the war against Japan. This was the first time Stalin made such a commitment. The main subject of discussion at this conference, however, was the question of the " second front " by the United States and Great Britain in Europe. Roosevelt and Churchill assured Stalin that an invasion of France would take place around May 1944 and that by July of that year a million men would be landed on French soil.

The official communique, issued on December first, stated that concerted plans for " the destruction of German forces " had been completed and that the Allies intended to work together in peace as well as in war. " We leave here, friends in fact, in spirit and in purpose," said the communique.

THE YALTA AGREEMENT

By the beginning of 1945 the defeat of Germany was imminent. The Allied landings in France, in June 1944, had been successful beyond expectations, and all France had been liberated. On the eastern front the Red Army had crossed the German border on August 18, 1944. Most of Germany's satellites had deserted her. Rumania had capitulated on August 23, followed by Bulgaria on September 9 and Finland on September 19. Hungary held out until January 20, 1945. The final assaults on Germany were imminent, and it was apparent that Germany, which had been bled white, could hold out only a few months longer.

In a message to the Congress on January 6, 1945 President Roosevelt outlined the favorable progress of the war and emphasized that many more desperate battles remained to be fought before Germany would be defeated. He defended the Administration's strategy of not having directed the major part of American power against the Japanese and of having instead fought with equal intensity on both European and Pacific battle areas. He reminded the Congress of the debt we owed to the two " indomitable " European allies, Russia and Britain. " Nor can we forget how, for more than seven long years," he said, " the Chinese people have been sustaining the barbarous attack of the Japanese and containing large enemy forces on the vast areas of the Asiatic mainland."

Early in February Roosevelt arrived in Yalta, on the Crimean peninsula, to confer with Stalin and Churchill on final war plans. China was not represented. He was accompanied by Secretary Stettinius, James Byrnes, and high ranking military officers. Roosevelt was no longer a well man. Moreover, the diplomatic position of the United States vis-a-vis the Soviet Union was now extremely weak. Russian troops were in occupation of all eastern Europe and Stalin had never made any commitments concerning the restoration of prewar frontiers in eastern Europe and the Balkans. In addition, Stalin was in a most favorable position to exact further concessions in return for taking Russia into the war against Japan.

The official communique of the conference, issued on February 11, stated that general agreement had been reached on the convening of a conference at San Francisco in April for the establishment of a United Nations peace organization, on plans for the definitive defeat of Germany, and on common plans and policies for enforcing unconditional surrender terms on Germany. The communique also announced that machinery would be established for the regular consultation of the foreign ministers of the Big Three powers. Declarations were also made concerning liberated

Europe which pledged that Nazism and Fascism would be extirpated and that the liberated peoples would be given the opportunity to organize interim governments broadly representative of all democratic elements. Faith was reaffirmed in the high principles of the Atlantic Charter.

Not until the war was over, a year later, did the American people learn of additional secret arrangements made at Yalta affecting the Far East. This communique was not released with the original communique because it contained provisions detrimental to China and also because it disclosed Russian intentions toward Japan, with whom Russia remained technically at peace and bound by a non-aggression treaty. This communique, released on February 11, 1946, disclosed that agreement had been reached on the maintenance of the status quo in regard to the People's Republic of Outer Mongolia. This republic was a Communist satellite of Russia; the agreement therefore recognized that Outer Mongolia was irretrievably lost to China, to whom it had once belonged as a dependency, and that it was to remain in the Soviet orbit. Even more significantly, substantial concessions were made to Russia at the direct expense of China. The port of Dairen was to be internationalized, with the " preeminent " interests of the Soviet Union recognized; Port Arthur was to be leased to Russia as a naval base; the Chinese Eastern Railroad and the South Manchurian Railroad were to be placed under joint Sino-Russian management; and China was to be restored to sovereignty over Manchuria, but with the " preeminent " interests of Soviet Russia recognized. In addition, Russia was to receive from Japan the southern half of Sakhalin and all of the Kurile Islands. In return for these far-reaching concessions, Soviet Russia promised to enter the war against Japan within two to three months after the final defeat of Germany and to permit the establishment of American bases in the immediate future at Komsomolsk and Nikolaevsk, and later at Kamchatka.

The Yalta arrangements concerning East Asia have been the subject of acrimonious debate in America ever since they became known to the public. Some have argued that they represent a " sell-out " to Soviet Russia that was needless and unjustified since Japan was practically beaten. Others, however, have strongly defended them. They have argued that competent opinion at the time was divided on whether or not Japan was near capitulation, that Japan was believed to have powerful forces stationed in Manchuria, and that it was thought the concessions made to secure Russian entrance in the war would result in the saving of thousands of American lives. They have further offered the argument that Russia would have taken the concessions anyway.

Shortly after his return to Washington, the President on March second discussed the Yalta conference before a joint session of the Congress. Omitting any reference to the secret and unpublished agreement concerning East Asia, he claimed that " more than ever before the major allies are closely united " and that " the ideal of lasting peace will become a reality." He predicted that the Yalta Conference " marked the end of the system of unilateral action and exclusive alliances and spheres of influences and balances of power and all other expedients that have been tried for centuries and have always failed." It might be pointed out, however, that Roosevelt was not alone in his hopes and enthusiasm for Big Three unity and cooperation in the " peace " that was to come. Most of the American press shared his enthusiasm and hopes. Typical of press comments at that time was the prediction of *Time Magazine* that " all doubts about the Big Three's ability to co-operate in peace as well as in war seem now to have been swept away."[1]

Two months later the ailing President was dead. He was succeeded by the vice-president, Harry S. Truman. Up to this point he had generally been regarded as only a minor politician, but the nation to a man wished him well in the herculean task of pulling together all the threads of the wartime skein. Needless to say, no president ever inherited more portentous unfinished business.

THE SURRENDER OF JAPAN

On the very day that President Roosevelt delivered his last message to the Congress, the Allied armies were driving on relentlessly to the final and definitive victory in Europe. On March 5 Allied troops entered Cologne; by the beginning of April Russian troops had entered Warsaw, Budapest and Vienna. On April 25 American and Russian troops linked at Torgau in central Germany. On May first the death of Hitler was proclaimed, and on the following day Russian troops entered the smoldering ruins of Berlin. German armies were now surrendering helter skelter. For a moment it appeared that there might not be any government in Germany to accept formally the surrender terms and give cease fire orders. A de facto government was organized, however, headed by Admiral Dönitz and General Jodl, which on May 7 accepted the terms of unconditional surrender. The following day was proclaimed V-E, or victory in Europe, day. The war in Europe was over and Germany was a vast ruin, her cities smoldering and littered with rubble and death.

Meanwhile, in the Pacific area the Japanese forces had also been suffering a series of catastrophic defeats. Saipan had been captured by American forces in June 1944, and from bases on that island regular air raids were launched on the Japanese home islands. A week later a decisive naval battle was fought in Philippine waters in which fleets commanded by Admirals William Halsey and Thomas C. Kincaid practically annihilated the remnants of the Japanese fleet, sinking or damaging fifty-eight Japanese warships. Japanese resistance on the Philippines was then rapidly overcome, and preparations were rushed for the final knockout blows against the Japanese home islands. On March 20 Iwo Jima was captured. In April American troops landed on Okinawa and fought savagely until mid-June before overcoming the stubbornly resisting Japanese. The proximity of these islands to Japan made it possible to launch devastating air raids over strategic and heavily populated areas. By the middle of summer the great industrial centers of Japan had been subjected to shattering air raids that wiped out huge industrial areas and severely crippled industrial production. Meanwhile, the Japanese fleet had been practically annihilated and the economy had been reduced to dependence on stockpiles and inadequate indigenous resources. While a large part of Japan's industrial establishment was still capable of producing war materials, the increasing shortages of critically needed raw materials and the disordered state of the economy made it apparent to even the most stubborn Japanese that the economic means of continuing the war were almost exhausted.

With the war in Europe over and victory clearly in sight in the Far East, President Truman journeyed to Potsdam, in Germany, to participate in the last great wartime conference of the Allied powers. At Potsdam, on July 17, he began discussions with Marshal Stalin and Clement Attlee, the new Prime Minister of Great Britain, who was assisted by the outgoing Winston Churchill, whose Conservative Party had just been repudiated at the polls. The Chinese Government was not represented, and it was allegedly informed by dispatch of the discussions affecting Far Eastern matters. The principal topics discussed by the heads of state were the conduct of the war in the Far East, the occupation of Germany, and the settlement of problems of international concern in the liberated countries of Europe.

With regard to the Far East, the United States, Great Britain and China in a thirteen-point proclamation issued on July 26, and officially known as the Potsdam Proclamation, warned Japan of the impending might which would soon be unleashed in all its fury unless capitulation was immediately offered. The proclamation ominously warned that " The prodigious land, sea and air forces of the United States, the British Empire and China, many times reinforced by their armies and fleets from the West, are poised to strike the final blows upon Japan." The proclamation stipulated the primary conditions which the Allies intended to impose upon Japan and made it clear that Japan was to be placed under Allied occupation until a new order was established. It insisted that all militarists and ultranationalists were " to be removed from authority and influence in Japan " and that all war criminals were to be speedily brought to trial. It further declared that Japan was to be completely demilitarized and that the Cairo Declaration was to be fully carried out, limiting Japan to the four main islands and such minor islands as might be designated by the Allies. The only alternative to acceptance of these terms, warned the proclamation, was " prompt and utter destruction."

Eleven days after the issuance of this stern proclamation, American aviators unleashed a devastating atomic bomb on Hiroshima which practically obliterated the entire city and killed or maimed tens of thousands of its 350,000 inhabitants. On August 9 another lethal atomic bomb crashed on Nagasaki, destroying a third of its industrial center and killing thousands.* On the preceding day, the Soviet Union had suddenly entered the war and begun the invasion of Manchuria, in violation of her non-aggression pact with Japan. Japan was now militarily prostrate and the frightful destruction and horror of the two atomic bombs convinced even the most fanatical militarists that continuation of the war was sheer folly. Peace feelers were put through the Swiss Government, and on August 14 Japan accepted the Potsdam Proclamation as a basis for unconditional surrender. As a matter of record, the Japanese had put forth strong peace feelers continuously since the beginning of the year, through the Vatican and the Soviet Union, but for some reason they had been coldly ignored by Washington.

Prior to the acceptance of the terms of unconditional surrender, the Japanese Government had stated that it was willing to accept the principles of the Potsdam Proclamation, provided " the said

---

* According to figures released by the Japanese Board of Economic Stabilization on April 7, 1949, one out of every three of Hiroshima's population and one out of every four of Nagasaki's population were either killed or injured by the atomic bombs.

declaration does not comprise any demand which prejudices the prerogatives of His Majesty as a Sovereign Ruler." Secretary of State James Byrnes, at the direction of President Truman and acting on behalf of the principle Allied powers, informed the Japanese Government that " From the moment of surrender the authority of the Emperor and the Japanese Government to rule the state shall be subject to the Supreme Commander of the Allied Powers who will take such steps as he deems proper to effectuate the surrender terms." On August 14, as indicated above, the Japanese offered to surrender without reservations, and President Truman then announced that the Japanese offer was " a full acceptance of the Potsdam Declaration* which specifies the unconditional surrender of Japan." The President also disclosed that General Douglas MacArthur had been appointed Supreme Commander for the Allied Powers to accept the formal Japanese surrender.[2]

Small units of an airborne division landed at Atsugi airport, outside battered Yokohama, during the last days of August and were courteously received by the Japanese. On September first the main forces of the United States Eighth Army began landing in strength around the Tokyo Bay area. On that day, also, the formal surrender ceremonies were held aboard the battleship *Missouri*. In the so-called Instrument of Surrender signed by the Japanese representatives,† Japan pledged unreserved acceptance of and compliance with the Potsdam Proclamation, unconditional surrender of all her armed forces, the liberation of all Allied prison-

---

* The Potsdam Proclamation has been referred to indiscriminately as both the Potsdam Proclamation and the Potsdam Declaration.

† The Instrument of Surrender was signed by General MacArthur as Supreme Commander for the Allied Powers; by Admiral Chester W. Nimitz as the representative of the United States; and by other representatives of nations that had been at war with Japan, which included China, Great Britain, the Soviet Union, Australia, Canada, the French Provisional Government, the Netherlands, and New Zealand. On the Japanese side, Mamoru Shigemitsu signed for the Government and General Umezu, for the Imperial Headquarters.

ers of war, and full acceptance of the authority of the Supreme Commander for the Allied Powers.

On the day the Instrument of Surrender was signed, the Emperor of Japan informed his people in an imperial rescript that he had authorized the Japanese Imperial Headquarters to sign on his behalf the Instrument of Surrender and that he desired his subjects to cease all hostilities and to comply faithfully with the surrender terms. On that same day President Truman also addressed the American people over the radio. He proclaimed September second as V-J Day (Victory in Japan Day) and reminded the nation that " We shall not forget Pearl Harbor." He warned of the difficult problems that lay ahead for the United States, but he optimistically opined that " Together with the United Nations it can build a world of peace founded on justice and fair dealing and tolerance."

CHAPTER VIII

THE OCCUPATION OF JAPAN

PROSTRATE JAPAN

The mass of rubble and debris produced by the awesome atomic blasts at Hiroshima and Nagasaki symbolized the abject crumbling of the once proud Japanese Empire. With the formal signing of the surrender terms aboard the battleship *Missouri*, a dramatic and tragic ending was written to the process which the Japanese had begun so cautiously and laboriously in the latter part of the nineteenth century. That process, begun with the peaceful annexation of the Ryukyus and the negotiated acquisition of the Kuriles, had gradually resulted in the establishment of a vast, rich and powerful empire which had enabled the Japanese to dominate all the approaches to China, to control Korea and Manchuria, and ultimately to occupy a large part of the extensive southwestern Pacific area. Even in the prewar period, this empire had enabled the Japanese to establish a strong and highly productive economy which made Japan the workshop and arsenal of Asia and moreover enabled her to challenge the economic systems of some of the most highly industrialized nations of the West.

With the signing of the surrender terms, however, Japan practically reverted to its territorial status of the early Meiji period, when it was confined to the islands of the Japanese archipelago. All that had been gained by conquest, and even what had been obtained peacefully, were lost to the Japanese nation. Gone were

JAPAN
AND THE
PEACE TREATY

■ CLAIMS AND TITLES RENOUNCED
BY JAPAN

Ⓐ CEDED TO RUSSIA

Ⓑ CONCURRENCE BY JAPAN IN ANY U.S.
PROPOSAL FOR A U.S. TRUSTEESHIP
UNDER THE UNITED NATIONS

Ⓒ CLAIMS AND TITLES RENOUNCED
BY JAPAN; JAPANESE ACCEPTANCE
OF UNITED NATIONS DECISION OF
APRIL 1947 ESTABLISHING A U.S.
TRUSTEESHIP

all the conquests of World War II; gone were Manchuria and Korea, Formosa, the Pescadores, southern Sakhalin and the Kuriles; gone even were the Ryukyus and the Bonins. Gone were the extensive raw materials of these areas which had been so vitally necessary for the functioning of Japan's highly industrialized economy geared to the survival needs of her teeming population.

With Japan's total defeat, moreover, the equilibrium of the entire Far East was bruskly upset, for in spite of her militarism and aggression Japan had been a strong, albeit a very selfish, stabilizing factor. With the total destruction of Japanese power, great power vacuums were created throughout Asia within which confusion and disorders arose. Soviet and American power and influence rushed into and clashed in these vacuums to give the "cold war" a concrete Far Eastern setting. Before a new balance of power could be created, China had arisen as a Communist state closely allied with Russia, Korea had been bathed in the blood of civil war, Southeastern Asia was thrown into confusion and warfare, and Communism had become the master of a vast Eurasian area stretching from eastern Europe to the South China Sea, within whose confines nearly a third of the human race was enclosed.

The occupation of Japan began officially on September 2, 1945. On that day the Japanese began a new chapter in their history. It was a chapter of military occupation and dictation from an alien power, of initial economic prostration and social chaos, of power helplessness in a world where power counted for more than ever before. On that day the Japanese awakened as if from a dream. They fully realized that the power of imperial Japan was fully shattered, that the divine descent of the Emperor and the alleged holy mission of their Empire were but myths, and that the task of reconstructing their rubble-strewn land was a hard and grievous burden. On that day Japan was friendless and alone. No people ever faced a grimmer future. Subsequent and rapidly moving developments were to bring new hope and opportunity to the Japanese, but at the time this was not foreseen by either the Japanese or their conquerors.

OCCUPATION POLICY AND ADMINISTRATION

Plans and policies for the occupation of Japan had been under consideration by the State Department as early as the spring of 1945. Initial proposals provided for the very harsh treatment of the Japanese people and the imposition of a type of " Morganthau Plan " which would practically destroy the Japanese industrial base and reduce the country to an agrarian economy. Thanks to the influence and intervention of former Ambassador Grew and others, these extreme proposals were greatly modified and general policies were adopted which took some realistic cognizance of the blamelessness and requirements of the Japanese people as a whole.

Late in August 1945 the United States suggested to China, Soviet Russia and Great Britain that a Far Eastern Advisory Committee (FEAC) be established which would consist of representatives of the powers that had participated in the war against Japan. It was proposed that this committee would make recommendations " on the formulation of policies, principles and standards " with which Japan would comply to meet her obligations in accordance with the surrender terms.[1] By this time, however, the wartime cooperation of the so-called " democratic nations " was over. Although Russia had fought Japan for only a week, she apparently was under the illusion that she might have an equal part with the United States in the occupation of Japan. Accordingly, she refused to become a member of the contemplated committee and argued that it would essentially be an advisory body and not, as she desired, a genuine control commission for the occupation of Japan. Despite this rebuff, the United States and the other nations concerned went forward with a study of problems dealing with Japanese disarmament, demilitarization and economic rehabilitation. Meanwhile, the United States clung to the hope that Russia's abstention would only be temporary, that Russia would recognize the realities of America's right to pre-eminence in the occupation, and that a compromise of some kind might be worked out.

A compromise was in effect reached at the Moscow Conference of Foreign Ministers on December 27, 1945. At this conference the foreign ministers of the principal allied powers agreed to replace the FEAC with a so-called Far Eastern Commission (FEC) and an Allied Control Council for Japan. Like the contemplated FEAC, the Far Eastern Commission was to be composed of representatives of all the powers that had fought against Japan, but provision was made for the inclusion of additional nations.* The primary position of the United States was tacitly recognized by the provision that the FEC was to hold its meetings in Washington. Concessions to the Russian viewpoint are apparent from the provisions which stipulated that the FEC was " to formulate the policies, principles and standards in conformity with which fulfillment by Japan of its obligations under the Terms of Surrender may be accomplished; " that it was to have authority to review any directive issued to the Supreme Commander of the Allied Powers or any action taken by him; and that all directives issued to the Supreme Commander were to be prepared by the United States in accordance with the policy decisions of the FEC. The primary and controlling position of the United States was assured, however, by the provision that it was authorized to prepare and issue interim directives to the Supreme Commander on all matters for which specific policy decisions by the FEC were lacking. American control was moreover fully assured by the simple, but highly significant fact, that the Supreme Commander received all his instructions and directives, including FEC policy decisions, from the United States government only.

---

* The following nations were originally represented in the FEC : the United States, the United Kingdom, the Soviet Union, China, France, the Netherlands, Canada, Australia, New Zealand, India and the Philippine Commonwealth.

The Allied Council for Japan was to hold its meetings in Tokyo and was to be comprised of the Supreme Commander or his deputy and representatives of Russia and China and one member to represent conjointly the United Kingdom, Australia, New Zealand and India. The council's functions were to be consultative and advisory only, but almost from the moment it began functioning in Tokyo the Soviet delegate attempted to exploit it for the purpose of denouncing the United States and its occupation policies and of spreading pro-Soviet propaganda. In actual operation the council served no useful or constructive purpose. Its meetings were characterized by constant strife and bickering between the Soviet and American delegates, and by the latter part of the occupation period it had practically ceased to function.

In the framing of American policy for Japan and other occupied areas, the State Department coordinated its efforts with the War and Navy departments. The need for a coordinated policy had been recognized in the closing months of the war, since Japan and other defeated enemy nations would be occupied and administered by American military forces. A State-War-Navy Coordinating Committee, commonly known as SWNCC, was accordingly established in the summer of 1945 to function as the coordinator of American policy for occupied areas. It consisted of representatives of the State, War and Navy departments and drew up policies which were submitted to the President for approval. Although the service departments were included, it was effectively controlled and dominated by the State Department. Policies drawn up by SWNCC and approved by the President were transmitted by the Joint Chiefs of Staff to the respective commanders in the occupied areas concerned.

On August 29, 1945 SWNCC issued a so-called United States Initial Post-Surrender Policy, which was " a statement of general initial policies relating to Japan after surrender." This document received the approval of the President and was immediately transmitted by the Joint Chiefs of Staff to General MacArthur. In general, it was an outline of basic American policy for occupied

Japan and elaborated upon the stipulations of the Potsdam Proclamation. It stipulated that the " ultimate objectives " of the United States during the initial period of the occupation were: (1) " to insure that Japan will not again become a menace to the United States or to the peace and security of the world," and (2) " to bring about the eventual establishment of a peaceful and responsible government which will support the objectives of the United States as reflected in the ideals and principles of the Charter of the United Nations." It declared that while no support or favor would be given to the existing Imperial Government, it nevertheless would be utilized as a means of implementing occupation policies. This provision made it clear that the United States had no intention of destroying Japan's imperial system, as had been advocated by some fanatical Americans earlier in the year. The document further stipulated that Japan was to be completely disarmed and demilitarized; that all militarists and ultranationalists were to be purged and removed from positions of influence; and that all " war criminals " were to be brought to justice speedily. In the economic area, " the existing economic basis of Japanese military strength must be destroyed and not be permitted to revive." There was to be " a wide distribution of income and the ownership of the means of production and trade " and the large industrial and banking combines were to be dissolved. Japan was to make full reparations payments through the transfer of Japanese property located outside Japan and such goods or existing capital equipment as were not necessary for a peaceful Japanese economy or for the use of the occupation forces. " Full and prompt restitution " was to be made of all identifiable looted property, and all foreign-owned properties that had been confiscated in Japan were to be returned to their rightful owners.[2]

This policy was elaborated upon in a lengthy Basic Occupation Directive which was transmitted to the Supreme Commander by the Joint Chiefs of Staff early in November 1945 and by other directives transmitted from time to time throughout the occupation period.   Transmittals from the Joint Chiefs of Staff included policy suggestions as well as directives.   General MacArthur was allowed considerable latitude in the implementation of his directives, and he and his headquarters moreover greatly influenced many of the policy decisions that were made in Washington and then transmitted to him as formal directives.

The occupation of Japan began officially on September 2, 1945. The selection of MacArthur to head the occupation had been made as early as the beginning of August 1945.   On September 6 he was formally authorized by President Truman to act as Supreme Commander for the Allied Powers in the occupation of Japan. Broad and vast powers were implied in his instructions.   They stated explicitly that " the authority of the Emperor and the Japanese Government to rule the State is subordinate to you as Supreme Commander for the Allied Powers."   They further stipulated that the control and administration of Japan was to be exercised through the Japanese Government " to the extent that such an arrangement produces satisfactory results " and that the Potsdam Proclamation was to be given full effect since it formed a part of American policy " stated in good faith with relation to Japan and with relation to peace and security in the Far East."[3]

The first occupying forces to land in Japan were American.   In February 1946 contingents of British Commonwealth troops began arriving to occupy and administer the Kobe-Hiroshima area. These troops never numbered more than 45,000 and most of them were withdrawn by the spring of 1948.   No Russian, Chinese or other troops participated as occupying forces.   The military occupation of Japan was hence essentially an American occupation, in which American military forces comprised the bulk of the troop strength.   It was also fundamentally an American occupation from the standpoint of policies and control, for despite his euphemistic title of Supreme Commander for the Allied Powers, General MacArthur was appointed by, responsible to, and directed by the President of the United States through the Joint Chiefs of Staff.

The military occupation of Japan was accomplished peacefully, despite the fact that throughout September 1945 the armed Japanese forces on the home islands outnumbered the occupying forces perhaps as much as twenty to one. There were no clashes or incidents worthy of mention. Nor was there any apparent bitterness on the part of the Japanese people despite the shattering of their cities and the horror of the two atomic bombs. As a matter of record, most Japanese were friendly and within a few weeks considerable numbers of them actually came to believe that the Americans had come as liberators. From the moment the occupation began, General MacArthur and the occupation forces received a cooperation that was probably without precedent in the history of military occupations. This was largely due to the realism of the Japanese people, but it was also due to the command of the Emperor that the " new situation " should be gracefully accepted and to the traditional docility of the Japanese people to authority, whatever its source.

General MacArthur established his headquarters in the heart of Tokyo, and most of its remaining modern buildings were immediately requisitioned for occupation use. In order to carry out his vast occupation responsibilities, he established a number of staff sections, such as the Government Section, the Economic and Scientific Section, the Natural Resources Section, and the Civil Information and Education Section.* These sections were originally small and almost entirely staffed with military personnel, but civilian specialists in various fields were rapidly recruited to replace the military. The sections however remained headed by army officers (a few generals, but mostly colonels), and they were at all times strictly accountable to General MacArthur. Each of

---

* The other staff sections initially established were : Public Health and Welfare Section, Legal Section, International Prosecution Section, Civil Communications Section, Statistical and Reports Section, Counter-Intelligence Section, and the Diplomatic Section. This last-named section handled matters relating to Japan's relations with other countries. Unlike the other sections, it was under the direction of the State Department.

these sections soon mushroomed in size, in traditional bureaucratic fashion, into mighty little empires. Among the thousands of civilians that staffed them were many capable and conscientious specialists and workers, many of them inspired with a " mission complex," but far too many were maladjusted individuals and incompetents. It is probably safe to say that all necessary and desirable occupation functions could easily have been administered by a civilian force of less than a half of that which was recruited.

From their Tokyo headquarters, General MacArthur and his staff-section chiefs implemented policies formulated in Washington by means of written directives and oral instructions to the Japanese Government. So-called " military teams " were scattered throughout Japan for the purpose of checking up on Japanese compliance with the occupation directives and instructions. These military teams were under the initial direction of General Robert Eichelberger, Commander in Chief of the Eighth Army, with headquarters in Yokohama. Among many other reasons, the efficiency of the occupation was greatly reduced by the ignorance or very little knowledge of Japan and the Japanese on the part of most occupation officials. Poor administration also reduced its effectiveness. Directives and instructions poured out of headquarters in a continuous stream but in many, if not most, instances, there was no effective method or means of knowing to what degree the Japanese Government had actually complied with them and required their enforcement. By and large the Japanese Government cooperated honestly, to the extent of its ability to understand the intent of the directives and instructions received. In some instances, however, Japanese officials " played dumb," subtly sidetracked, or only partially complied with the directives and instructions.

ACCOMPLISHMENTS OF THE OCCUPATION

One of the first tasks to which General MacArthur gave his energetic attention was the disarming and demilitarization of

Japan so that it would be impossible for her again " to threaten the peace and security of the world." This task was carried out rapidly and enthusiastically. By the beginning of 1946 the task had almost been completed. On July 14, 1947 General Mac-Arthur triumphantly boasted that this assignment had been carried out so thoroughly by the occupation forces that " Japan could not rearm for modern war within a century." In view of the subsequent international developments which clearly revealed Russia and militant Communism as the gravest threats of the century to peace, this achievement came to haunt the United States, and with more than a considerable measure of cruel irony. Some consolation may be derived, however, by allowing for the oratorical prerogatives of General MacArthur and realizing that instead of " a century " he doubtless meant a generation or possibly not even more than a decade.

The so-called " war criminals " were rapidly rounded up and brought to trial. The trials fell into two main categories: (1) the trials of the Japanese individuals accused of having committed atrocities against military captives and civilians during the war, and (2) the trial of the so-called major " war criminals," such as General Tojo and former Foreign Minister Koki Hirota, who were accused of having plotted aggressions and violated solemn treaties. The trial of the major war criminals in Tokyo received the most publicity. It was dramatically staged, and dragged on until late in 1948, as if to demonstrate to the Japanese that the wheels of " democratic justice " grind slowly. General Tojo, Koki Hirota and several others were found guilty of the major counts against them and were executed in December of that year. Others, such as the former Foreign Minister Mamoru Shigemitsu, received long prison terms. None was completely acquitted.

Among those who judged these " war criminals " was a Soviet general, whose nation's crimes against humanity many times exceeded those of which the Japanese were accused. At any rate, most of the alleged crimes of which the Japanese defendants were accused are essentially ex post facto ones. History may honor the judgment of only one of the men who judged the Japanese. This man is Justice Pal of India. He issued a lengthy dissenting judgment which rejected the idea of ex post facto punishment and which in general is perhaps an extremely sound appraisal of whatever real guilt there is to be placed against Tojo and his co-defendants.

One of the most zealous of the early occupation projects was the great purge of all Japanese considered offensive to the United States in particular and to democracy in general. This colossal purge hit at hundreds of thousands of Japanese in all walks of life. It almost depleted the ranks of ability in educational, governmental and business fields. As the " cold war " with Russia grew hotter, and as it became apparent that Japan's industry could not recover to the extent desired by the United States, it began to be realized that the great purge was a mistake. Toward the close of the occupation, one of the principal objectives appeared to be that of " unpurging " the purged. By the time the occupation had officially terminated, almost all of those who had been purged had been restored to respectability.

The problem of democratizing Japan was handled like a great crusade, on paper at least. In October 1945 General MacArthur issued his famous civil liberties directive to the Japanese Government, which among other things ordered the release of all so-called political prisoners and required complete freedom of speech, organization and political action. Thanks to this directive all Communists, many of them hardened veterans of subversive propaganda and revolution, were released from the jails. Under the leadership of highly capable Japanese Communists who had returned from China, they were permitted to engage in unrestricted activities and bring about the establishment of the most powerful and most dangerous Communist movement in the history of Japan. Not until 1948 did General MacArthur fully awaken to the grave threat of Japanese Communism.

Early in January 1946 the Emperor was induced to renounce

all claims to divinity, and in the following year a new constitution was drawn up which contained some very advanced democratic concepts and principles. Despite the denials of occupation authorities, this constitution was essentially drafted by Americans, although it was ostensibly represented as being of Japanese creation, with Americans only offering " advice." One has only to read the constitution, even in English but preferably in Japanese, to appreciate how un-Japanese is its phraseology. It must be recognized as being a good constitution, however, and one of which any modern nation sincerely striving for the fulfillment of democracy could be proud.

One of the most unique features of this constitution is its renunciation of war and all types of military forces. This feature, of course, is an absurdity. Perhaps even stronger language is justified, for in a sense it has proven to be a criminal restriction in the face of the grave Chinese and Russian threats. That Japan should continue to abide by this myopic restriction in the face of the Communist threats must now be maddening to the millions of Americans who dig deeply to pay for armaments and who saw their husbands, sons and brothers whisked from their homes to serve on distant Korean battle-fields.

In the field of education and information media, the occupation authorities also changed many things in the name of democracy. Much that was done will stand; much will not. One of the outstanding achievements was the elevation of the status of women. All discriminations against them because of their sex were removed and they were given the franchise. This privilege they have exercised with considerable credit to themselves, and a sizable number of women have been elected to the Diet. Much was also done to bring about the establishment of a freer and more responsible press.

How well these and other far-reaching political and social reforms will work out remains for time to tell. However, since the Japanese had already had decades of experience in partial forms of democracy and representative government, there is reason to believe that Japan will become an oriental version and bulwark of Western democracy and representative government. This hope can easily be frustrated, however, if the Western nations, including the United States, again fail to appreciate that the survival of democracy in this modern age is dependent on a reasonably full and abundant life for the toiling masses as well as for those who govern and control. This means that the survival and healthy development of democracy in Japan is highly dependent on Japan's economic prosperity.

A number of sweeping economic reforms were attempted, some of which were quite revolutionary in nature. The great industrial and banking combines were rather effectively broken up and the former so-called zaibatsu strangle hold on the economy was eliminated. In the process much of the wealth of the presurrender industrialists and capitalists was confiscated, and many of them were reduced to a state of relative penury. A framework of anti-monopoly and fair-trade laws was established. The permanence of these changes will greatly depend on whether an economy of scarcity, such as is the Japanese, can prosper without some control over raw materials, imports, and production quotas. The occupation reformers, of course, completely overlooked this vitally important factor and conceived their reforming program in the image of that prevailing in the United States, which regulates an economy of the greatest abundance. However, by 1948 American business circles, on learning of what was being attempted in Japan, became incensed and vociferous. Thereafter General MacArthur apparently ordered a relaxation and retreat in the monopoly-smashing crusade.

An ambitious rural land reform program was brought to a successful conclusion. Tenantry was practically eliminated and millions of farmers were enabled to own their own farm lands. In the implementation of this program the large landowners were compelled to sell their lands at fixed prices far below the actual market value. However, there is not much farm land to be distributed in Japan, where only about 16 percent of the area is cultivable, and hence this perhaps laudable program has resulted in the creation of millions of tiny farms, most of which vary in size from one to three acres. Whether these atomized farms can survive the stresses and strains that lie ahead also remains to be seen. Nevertheless, one of the most encouraging things in Japan today is the " solidness " and political moderation of these propertied, toiling farmers. One may be justified in believing that these millions of small farmers will continually remain a potent and moderating influence on both the extreme Left and the extreme Right. At any rate, one can be sure that having once owned the good earth which they till with their own hands, they will not lightly relinquish it.

Former restrictions on labor activities were removed and a numerically large and relatively sound labor movement came into existence. With more than a measure of justification, General MacArthur boasted that he was the father of the Japanese labor movement. Extensive legislation was passed which improved working conditions in general and added protection and new dignity to the laboring man and woman. Heavy blows were struck at the exploitation of child labor and at " labor bosses," whose business it was to control, sell, and profit from the services of unskilled laborers. However, during the first two years of the occupation many radical practices and principles were injected into the labor movement that are offensive from an American standpoint. It is also to be noted that although the occupation authorities fostered the development of a huge labor movement, they failed almost entirely to make adequate provision for the training of labor leaders who would have an understanding of the obligations as well as the rights of labor. An even more serious omission, however, was the failure of General MacArthur's headquarters in the early years of the occupation to prevent the Communists from gaining a powerful hold on labor and the labor movement.

The task of rehabilitating the collapsed Japanese economy was an extremely difficult one, despite the hundreds of millions of dollars poured into Japan by the United States Government. Deprived of the once extensive empire which had been a source of vitally needed industrial raw materials and foodstuffs, the heavily populated Japanese home islands were required to feed a rapidly increasing population that was augmented by additional millions who were repatriated from the Asiatic mainland and many islands of the Pacific. Since the termination of the Pacific War the population had been increasing annually at a natural rate of nearly a million and a half.

Initially all Japanese foreign trade was under the strict control of General MacArthur's headquarters, whose permission was necessary for the export or import of any item. A strenuous effort was made, nevertheless, to revive Japanese foreign trade so as to enable the Japanese to exchange manufactured goods for foodstuffs and raw materials. Efforts in this direction were not particularly successful at first, and by the summer of 1949 Japanese foreign trade was only a small portion of what it had been immediately before the war or even during the 1930–1934 period. During the first three years of the occupation, Japan's industrial potential was moreover only partly utilized because of the lack of raw materials, the economic dislocation that persisted, and the large numbers of skilled workers who were either unemployed or only partially employed. After the outbreak of the Korean War in the summer of 1950 the Japanese economy received an unexpected stimulus, and shortly thereafter exports rose sharply and at a monthly rate amounting to about a billion dollars annually. By 1953 exports approached the billion and a half dollar mark.

THE CHANGE IN OCCUPATION EMPHASIS

The occupation had begun essentially as a punitive one whose main purpose was to bring about the establishment of a Japan which would have neither the means nor the will to rearm and again threaten the peace of the Far East or the world. For more than two years General MacArthur's headquarters zealously carried out its Washington orders to mete out " just " punishment to all those who had in any way contributed to the building of a powerful and militaristic Japan. While there was also the Messianic objective of fostering the healthy growth of democracy, it was decidedly secondary to the primary objective. It was also apparently believed by many in Washington, and in the Tokyo occupation headquarters, that the development of a strong democracy would contribute toward the establishment of a militarily weak, anti-militaristic and peace-loving nation which might of its own weight serve to prevent the re-creation of a war machine or the reappearance of powerful economic empires that might serve as a support and base for resurgent militarism.

By the beginning of 1947, however, the occupation was beginning to become transformed into a benevolent tutelage and guardianship. This very significant change was primarily the result of two principal factors: (1) the radically changed international situation which had brought into existence a " cold war " between the powerfully armed Soviet Union and the United States, and (2) the general cooperation and goodwill manifested by most of the Japanese people and their officials. To many Americans it seemed like common sense to handle the occupation in such a manner that the Japanese people might be cultivated to become potential allies or at least friendly non-belligerents in case of a future war with Russia. Other Americans, however, continued to be obsessed with the wartime phobia against Japan. They persisted in feeling that the Japanese were not to be trusted and that nothing should be done to enable them to re-establish a strong economic base which might again be utilized for militaristic and aggressive purposes.

Despite this division of thought among Americans at that time, Washington began modifying the ultimate objectives of its policies and after 1947 the occupation became increasingly more benevolent. After December 1948 Washington policy required strenuous efforts to bring about the stabilization of the Japanese economy and to increase production to the highest levels possible. Previously General MacArthur had been required to maintain production only at a level adequate to prevent starvation, disease and unrest. With the change in policy, MacArthur's headquarters began turning over to the Japanese Government an increasing amount of control and authority over its foreign trade and internal affairs. Fraternization was now encouraged, and it increased with each passing month of the occupation. One unanticipated result of the long occupation period was that large numbers of Americans and Japanese came to know each other well for the first time, and in general they liked each other.

As 1949 drew to a close, however, there were increasing signs that the Japanese people were becoming restive under the long occupation whose termination was not then in sight. For most Japanese, particularly those living in the cities, life remained hard and difficult. The nation was still a long way from the goal of reasonable economic self-sufficiency, and it was feared that the possible withdrawal of American financial support might result in increased economic distress and perhaps even hunger. Hampered by the bureaucratic regulations and red tape of the occupation and a very considerable amount of impracticable and misdirected occupation idealism, not to mention more than a measure of occupation ineptness and bungling, Japanese businessmen were losing initiative and incentives for increasing economic production. Inflation continued its mad upward swirl. The black market continued to thrive and many Japanese were finding it more desirable and profitable to engage in the activities of this market than to participate in legitimate undertakings. A large part of the stable, cultured and "respectable" prewar middle class was ruined, and a new bourgeoisie of black marketeers and unscrupulous opportunists had arisen.

General MacArthur's own words to the effect that any occupation which lasted more than three years would invite failure were coming home to roost. With unrest and discontent increasing, the well organized and highly disciplined Communists began

increasing their influence and power among the discontented.
Nevertheless, while many Japanese were becoming disillusioned
and dissatisfied with the continuance of the occupation, they
were not as a result of their own thinking becoming anti-American.
They were fundamentally reacting as normal human beings.
They had complied with every provision of the Potsdam Proclamation; they had eagerly and enthusiastically absorbed the
precepts and principles of the democracy that the occupation
authorities had disseminated among them.   They had even of
their own initiative engaged in a searching and far-reaching
criticism of themselves and of the actions of their leaders since the
Meiji period.   Now they were longing for the opportunity to be
really free, to be able to call their land, poor as it might be, their
own.   No matter how benevolent, any occupation is an occupation and even the most docile and open-minded will eventually
tire of it.

With the outbreak of the Korean War in late June 1950 and the
entrance of Communist China in this conflict, an entirely new
feeling arose in Japan, which had long had a strong anti-Com-
munist bias.   The United States and its occupying forces were
now looked upon as protective agents of Japan.   Without arms,
without armed forces, without even the means of producing war
materials, most Japanese now realistically recognized that only
the United States stood between them and probable Communist
invasion.   Whereas formerly a very large number of responsible
Japanese had been in favor of complete American withdrawal,
army and all, most of the responsible and non-Leftist elements
now favored the maintenance of close relations with the United
States, the granting of military bases, and the stationing of
American troops on Japanese soil for an indefinite period.

The shocking Communist invasion of South Korea, coming
as the defiant culmination of a series of Communist aggressions,
together with the known preparedness of Russia's powerful
military machine to launch a devastating drive through western
Europe, also produced a profound change in American thinking.

By 1951 most Americans had come around to the realization that their country and civilization were in grave peril and that armaments and preparedness counted for more than ever before in history. Most Americans accordingly came to the view that Japan was the only truly stabilizing factor remaining in the Far East with the necessary potential to exercise an effective role in the desperate struggle to contain militant Communism. The changed attitude on the part of the American public was reflected in the revised policy of the State Department which favored the rearmament and remilitarization of Japan. Some of the Pacific nations, particularly Australia and the Philippines, were horrified at the thought of Japan possibly being permitted to build up military forces even for defensive purposes. Despite the outspoken opposition of these nations, the State Department persisted in its policy of cultivating Japan as a future ally and encouraging her government to take, of its own initiative, the necessary measures for the adequate defense of Japan.

THE REMOVAL OF GENERAL MACARTHUR

On April 11, 1951 General MacArthur was removed from his position as Supreme Commander for the Allied Powers and replaced by General Matthew B. Ridgway. In removing General MacArthur, President Truman had been prompted by differences with the general concerning the conduct of the war then raging in Korea rather than by differences on occupation policy. President Truman was also apparently motivated by what he considered to be the habitual " insubordination " of General MacArthur, a military commander, to himself, the commander in chief of the armed forces and the head of the civilian government of the United States.

For more than five and a half years General MacArthur had administered Japan with an iron hand and a Messianic zeal. When he had set foot on the smoldering ruins of Japan he had behind him the bitter memories of galling humiliations suffered

during the early months of the war and of long campaigns
savagely fought across a large part of the Pacific. Yet from the
moment he took command of the occupation there was no
bitterness in him; only the deep consciousness of a great mission
to be fulfilled in the pages of history. Throughout his administration, his iron rule was consistently tempered with justness and
understanding. How well he fulfilled what he apparently believed
to be a divine mission to transform Japan into his conception of
a democracy will be told objectively by the passing of time.

We are still too close to General MacArthur and the occupation
to attempt any evaluation that may have lasting validity. No
such attempt is herein made. However, certain facts must not
be lost from sight. As the administrator of occupied Japan,
General MacArthur had vast powers. At least until 1950, if not
later, he was in a position to influence and even to mold the
occupation policy which was made in Washington, as well
as to implement it in Japan with considerable latitude. From his
headquarters in Tokyo he had absolute control over his staff
sections, their personnel, and the implementation of their programs. If the successes of the occupation can be rightfully
accredited to him, then by the same yardstick he must be assessed
responsibility for its failures, its waste, and its incompetence,
wherever these may be recognized as having actually existed.

With Ridgway's replacement of MacArthur, the process of
dissolving the occupation and paving the way for Japan's return
to sovereignty and for possible post-treaty cooperation with the
United States was accelerated. Whereas General MacArthur
had somewhat isolated himself from the Japanese and had restricted himself to trips between his official residence at the
American Embassy building to his headquarters in the stately
Dai Ichi building of downtown Tokyo, about a mile away,
General Ridgway unobtrusively made himself seen around Japan
and made an earnest effort to know the Japanese and to familiarize
himself at first hand with their problems. Much of the fanfare
that had characterized the occupation disappeared almost over-

night and most occupation officials made some attempt to emulate the democratic example set by General Ridgway. These things were noticed by the Japanese of goodwill and they created a favorable impression. However, the pompousness and condescension of former days, not to mention the overbearing attitude and galling incompetence of too many officials who had lorded it over the proud and sensitive Japanese, had already scattered some seeds which were being sedulously cultivated by irresponsible Japanese extremists.

On April 30, 1952 General Mark Clark was appointed to succeed General Ridgway as Far Eastern commander. The latter was transferred to Paris to head the critically important North Atlantic Treaty Organization. By that time, however, the occupation had officially terminated, two days previously, as a result of the prescribed treaty ratifications having been exchanged.

THE CONCLUSION OF THE PEACE TREATY

The State Department had been considering a peace treaty for Japan as early as 1947. In July of that year it formally proposed that the thirteen member states of the Far Eastern Commission begin discussions on a peace treaty for Japan. The Soviet Union countered with the proposal that the Council of Foreign Ministers was the proper organ to discuss such a treaty. This council was composed of the foreign secretaries of Russia, the United States, Great Britain and France. It had come into existence in the closing period of World War II and the Soviet Union had continually exercised a powerful voice in its deliberations and decisions. Supported by Great Britain and France, however, the United States rejected the Russian proposal.

Not much further progress was made in the direction of a peace treaty until after the Chinese Communists had completed their conquest of China in October 1949. As a result of this ominous development, the position of the United States in the Far East was further weakened and Japan assumed increasingly greater importance as a potential and necessary collaborator. The key importance of Japan was made clear by Secretary of State Dean Acheson in a speech of January 1950.

In June 1950, immediately prior to the outbreak of the Korean War, John Foster Dulles visited Japan as the special representative of President Truman to exchange views with Japanese officials on the contemplated peace treaty. The worsening international situation speeded up the treaty-negotiating process. Serious treaty discussions got under way in the spring of 1951 when Dulles conferred with officials in Japan, the Philippines, Australia and New Zealand, and then in England and France. By the time he returned to the United States, in mid-June, the terms of a draft treaty had been completed almost in final form. This draft treaty contained quite generous treatment for Japan. Although she was to remain stripped of all her conquests and acquisitions since the Meiji period, no provision was made for reparations payments, no restriction was placed on rearmament, and no limitations were placed on foreign trade or industrial expansion.

Substantial accord had been reached between the United States and Great Britain and France on the terms of the treaty, but the Philippines, Australia and New Zealand expressed considerable dissatisfaction. Since Australia and New Zealand had been threatened by Japanese invasion during the war, these two countries naturally feared a rebirth of Japanese militarism and a possible recrudescence of Japanese aggression. Largely to placate these fears, the United States in July concluded a tripartite defense pact with Australia and New Zealand. The Filipinos, who had suffered more war damage than any other Asiatic people except the Chinese, were particularly bitter because the draft treaty made no provision for reparations payments by Japan. Dulles took a firm stand on reparations, however, and insisted that Japan was in no position to make reparations payments and that if such payments were forced upon Japan they would most

likely have to be financed indirectly by the American taxpayer.*
From its refuge on the island of Formosa, the beaten government
of Nationalist China also expressed dissatisfaction: not because
of the generous provisions of the draft treaty, but because it was
not being permitted to become a party to it. On the other hand,
the government of Communist China, in Peking, loudly insisted
that it alone was entitled to speak for the Chinese people with
regard to the peace treaty. The United States surmounted this
problem temporarily by taking the position that for the time
being neither the Nationalists nor the Chinese Communists would
be asked to participate in any Japanese peace treaty. Soviet
Russia, of course, maliciously continued its policy of obstruction.
It denounced Dulles and the draft treaty, gave no indication at
all of wishing to become a party to it, and supported Communist
China in its claim for participation in the treaty making.

In the middle of August Soviet Russia made the surprise
announcement that delegates would be sent to the forthcoming
peace conference, which was to be held in San Francisco. The
Russian change seemed to indicate the intention of continuing
the obstructionist tactics at San Francisco rather than a desire to
accept the treaty as it stood. At any rate, the United States made
it clear that the San Francisco conference was being called merely
to sign the treaty as it stood and not to reopen discussions concerning its provisions.

On August 26 India took an unanticipated stand when she
announced that no delegation would be sent to San Francisco.
India took the position that the Ryukyu and Bonin islands should
be returned to Japan and that military bases and the right of
stationing troops in Japan should not be granted to the United
States until after the treaty had been ratified and Japan had in
fact become a free and sovereign state. India did not propose
that Russia should also return southern Sakhalin and the Kuriles

---

* Incensed by the firmness of Dulles, some of the more intemperate Filipinos vented their ire by having him burned in effigy in Manila.

to Japan. Her stand on these territories was based on the argument that since they had been committed to Russia by the United
States and Britain in a solemn agreement freely made at Yalta
in 1945, India as a matter of basic policy could not advocate the
violation of an agreement that had been made in good faith by
the parties concerned. The Indian attitude greatly displeased
the United States, and at the same time helped to foster the impression that a large part of Asia was dissatisfied with the draft
treaty. Distasteful as was the Indian position to the United
States, it nevertheless represented an honest Indian viewpoint
and was in no way influenced by or connected with the Russian
tactics of obstruction.

The representatives of 52 nations convened in San Francisco
as planned, early in September, to sign the peace treaty. The
final form of the treaty was extremely generous, and might well
serve as a model for all treaties imposed by victors on the vanquished. Most of the credit for its high statesmanship must, of
course, go to its principal architect, John Foster Dulles. It did
not include any " war guilt " clause or any reference to the causes
of, or responsibility for, the tragic holocaust. Hence the absurd
error of the Versailles Treaty with its " war guilt " clause was
not repeated. The treaty recognized the principle of Japan's
obligation to make reparations payments to the nations which
had suffered from her aggressions, but it did not prescribe any
specified payments and moreover recognized that any payments
made should be of such a nature as not to injure the struggling
Japanese economy. Absolutely no restrictions of any kind were
placed on her industrial or trade expansion and the way was open
for her to compete freely for raw materials and markets. No
prohibitions were imposed on rearmament and remilitarization
or the right of belligerency. Nevertheless, Japan was deprived
of all her territorial acquisitions since the Meiji era. Among the
regions lost which had once been integral parts of the empire
as early as 1905 were the Ryukyu and Bonin island groups, as
well as the Kuriles and southern Sakhalin. It is not unlikely that

as soon as international conditions warrant, the United States may return the Ryukyus and Bonins (currently under American control). The Kurile Islands and southern Sakhalin are doubtless permanently lost to Japan, however, unless Russia is forced by arms to return them. History does not record any Russian habit of willingly relinquishing lands that have once been acquired.

On September 5 President Truman personally addressed the delegates assembled in San Francisco. He expressed great satisfaction with the treaty and urged the delegates to sign it. He stressed that it was " a treaty of reconciliation, which looks to the future, not the past." He pointed out that it was " fair to both victor and vanquished " and that it did not " contain the seeds of another war." He warmly congratulated the Japanese people for having complied with all the surrender terms and for having fully cooperated in carrying out the objectives of the occupation. " Let us be free of hate and malice," he pleaded, " to the end that from here on there shall be neither victors nor vanquished among us, but only equals in the partnership of peace."[4]

As had been anticipated, Andrei Gromyko, the Russian delegate, disparaged the treaty and reiterated the hackneyed accusation that the United States was contributing to the resurgence of Japanese militarism. The Polish and Czechoslovak delegates also castigated the treaty and impugned the good faith of the United States.[5] Other delegates, however, expressed satisfaction with the conciliatory and magnanimous nature of the treaty. Prime Minister Yoshida, the head of the Japanese delegation, made a magnificent and apparently very sincere speech for his nation. He gratefully recognized that the treaty was one of conciliation rather than vengeance, and he opined that it merited the " overwhelming support of my nation." He expressed regret that some of the delegates of the " free nations " were dissatisfied with some aspects of the treaty, but he pertinently pointed out that no multilateral treaty, including this one, could possibly satisfy everyone. Generous as was the treaty, however, he informed the delegates that even Japan had reason to be grieved by some of its provisions, specifically those which deprived Japan of sovereignty over the Kuriles, the Bonins, the Ryukyus and southern Sakhalin. He alluded to the strong desire of Japan to become a member of the United Nations and to contribute to her own defense to the extent that her resources permitted. No one should fear any Japanese move in the direction of self-defense, he argued, for Japan no longer had either the means or the will to engage in aggression. He eloquently promised that "We are determined to take our place among the nations who are dedicated to peace, to justice, to progress and freedom, and we pledge ourselves that Japan shall play its full part in striving toward these ends."[6]

On September 8 the representatives of 49 nations signed the peace treaty. The representatives of the three Communist states present at the conference (Russia, Poland and Czechoslavakia) boycotted the signing. Two important Asiatic nations, India and Burma, did not sign as they had not sent representatives. The treaty was to come into effect when it was ratified by Japan and the United States and any seven of thirteen specified nations which had played a major part in the war against Japan.

On that same day, Japan and the United States also signed a security pact which provided that with the coming into force of the peace treaty the United States was to station "land, air and sea forces in and about Japan." The pact further stipulated that Japan "will itself increasingly assume responsibility for its own defense against direct and indirect aggression."[7] The obvious purpose of the pact was for the United States to assume responsibility for the defense of Japan against possible Russian or Chinese aggression until Japan was in a position to do so herself.

For the purpose of defining the terms and conditions under which the United States would be granted leases and facilities for the fulfillment of its obligations in accordance with the security pact, Japan and the United States concluded an administrative agreement on February 28, 1952, at the Japanese Foreign Office. While this agreement conferred on security forces and their dependents a considerable number of extraterritorial privileges, it nevertheless stipulated that " It is the duty of members of the United States armed forces, the civilian component, and their dependents to respect the law of Japan and to abstain from any activity inconsistent with the spirit of this Agreement."[8]

EMERGENT SOVEREIGN JAPAN

In the meantime, General Ridgway had been dissolving the occupation in an orderly manner. By early 1952 the administration of the occupation had been greatly simplified and occupation personnel had been reduced to a mere core. Extensive powers had been returned to the Japanese Government, and the occupation was functioning more in a " clean up " and advisory role than in a directing one. Large numbers of American military forces remained stationed on the islands, however, and work was accelerated on the completion of installations at bases for the adequate accommodation and utilization of sizable forces for the defense of Japan in accordance with the terms of the security pact.

As the end of the occupation came in sight, Japan appeared to be relatively stable and to have made an impressive comeback from the ruin of total defeat. American financial assistance amounting to well over two billion dollars and the hard work and perseverance of the Japanese, aided by the economic stimulus of the Korean War, had resulted in a very substantial expansion of production and exports. By 1953 industrial production surpassed that of the 1932–36 period by about 40 percent, and the standard of living was estimated to almost equal that of any prewar year. Imports amounted to more than two billion dollars and they were more than balanced by merchandise and invisible exports. Nevertheless, there was a feeling of great uneasiness among the Japanese people, which was largely based on the fear that the " prosperity " was transient and dependent on the procurement orders for the United Nations forces fighting in Korea.

The more optimistic Japanese held to the hope that Japan might play a principal role in the economic reconstruction of Korea, when peace came to that devastated land, and that Japan might regain extensive markets in areas characterized by low per capita purchasing power, particularly in Southeast Asia.

CHAPTER IX

SOVEREIGN JAPAN AND THE FUTURE

THE ROAD TO NORMALCY

On April 28, 1952 the San Francisco Peace Treaty came into full effect as a result of the necessary ratifications, and the long occupation was officially terminated. Robert Murphy became the first American ambassador to postwar Japan, and Eikichi Araki became the first postwar Japanese ambassador to the United States. Each was eminently qualified for his difficult assignment, and each faced the challenging problems of his position with enthusiasm, understanding and tact.

Within a year, on April 2, 1953, a Treaty of Friendship, Commerce and Navigation was signed at the Japanese Foreign Office by Foreign Minister Katsuo Okazaki and Ambassador Murphy. The treaty was to become effective one month after the exchange of ratifications and was to remain in effect for a minimum of ten years, after which it was to continue in effect until and unless terminated by either party with one-year's notice. This treaty replaced the former Commercial Treaty of 1911 which had been denounced by the United States in the summer of 1940. It provided for most-favored-nation treatment for the nationals of each country and in general contained provisions designed to facilitate the development of broad commercial relations.

As Japan took her place among the free and sovereign nations, control of the country appeared to be firmly in the hands of the moderate elements under the leadership of the conservative Liberal Party of Prime Minister Yoshida. Communism and extremism appeared to have been eliminated as serious threats to a middle-of-the-road policy. Many genuine liberals feared, however, that the " reinvigorated democracy " of Japan rested on tenuous and unstable foundations and that the reactionaries and ultra-nationalists were grave potential dangers who were craftily maneuvering for the " psychological time " when they might again usurp power in the near future.

Although the occupation had terminated as a very benevolent one, there nevertheless arose a considerable and alarming amount of anti-Americanism. That some anti-Americanism should have arisen as a result of the crushing defeat of war and the humiliation of occupation was to be expected, of course, from a people with the pride, traditions and long history of the Japanese. That the anti-Americanism attained the extent it did, however, was un-anticipated, and also quite unmerited. One need not search far for the causes of this " excessive and unwarranted " anti-Ameri-canism. They are to be found principally in the opportunistic tactics of the extreme Leftists, especially the Communists, and some irresponsible Rightists who were now beginning to come out partially into the open. For the Communists in particular the presence of large numbers of American security forces on Japanese soil and the continued cooperation of the Yoshida government with the United States was a deterrent, if not an insurmountable obstacle, to any calculated or reckless attempt to usurp control of the country. Irresponsible Rightists, many of whom now began to dream of " the glorious old days of imperial Japan," not only contributed to the perpetua-tion of anti-American fabrications, but some of them even co-operated and connived with Leftist extremists in their dissemina-tion.

Despite the existence of a dangerous amount of anti-American sentiment, the solid mass of the Japanese people, when left to its own thinking and inclinations, harbored no particular animosity toward the United States.* On the contrary, it seemed to favor the Yoshida policy of continued cooperation with the United States and apparently felt that Japanese-American cooperation was to the mutual advantage of both peoples. Intellectuals and political opportunists, especially the extremists, were nevertheless bombarding this solid mass with propaganda, some of it outrightly vicious, and some of it extremely subtle but no less vicious. It is as easy to exaggerate the extent of post-treaty anti-Americanism in Japan as it is to underestimate it. It would be well to bear in mind that the solid mass of the Japanese citizenry is basically not much different than the solid mass in other countries: it is preoccupied with the difficult problem of earning a living and has precious little time or energy for dreaming of or imagining alleged wrongs committed by Americans and their government at the expense of Japan.

THE PROBLEM OF THE SECURITY FORCES

Among the many immediate post-treaty problems that confronted the United States and Japan, four are of particular significance and delicacy: (1) the problem of the American security forces stationed in Japan; (2) the problem of extraterritoriality; (3) the problem of Japanese rearmament; and (4) the problem of Japan's economic survival.

In accordance with the terms of the Mutual Defense Pact which had been concluded contemporaneously with the San Francisco Peace Treaty, large numbers of American military forces were stationed in Japan at stipulated bases. These forces were intended to be stationed in Japan primarily for the defense of Japan against external threats. While these threats were not

---

* By "solid mass of the Japanese people" is meant that very large segment of the population (independent farmers, small businessmen and home enterprisers, white-collar workers, etc.) which comprises between two-thirds and three-quarters of the total population.

specifically named, they were clearly understood to be Russia primarily and China secondarily.

Although a majority of the Japanese favored the presence of these American forces, serious problems arose from their presence which, when exploited by irresponsible and reckless extremists, complicated and made much more difficult the problem of placing Japanese-American relations on a sound basis. Among the welter of accusations made which had some, albeit slight, validity, were the following: (1) the leasing of sizable areas of land for bases and maneuvers deprived the land-starved people of valuable acreage which was needed for food production; (2) the immorality which festered around the military bases endangered public morals and the sex crimes committed by American soldiers outraged the public's sensibilities; (3) drivers of military vehicles endangered the life and limb of Japanese civilians, and security force offenders invariably remained unpunished for traffic offenses or got off easily; (4) military maneuvers, artillery practice and flights of military planes disturbed students and interfered with fishermen and farmers.[1] Even these accusations, however, hardly merit rebuttal since in general they are concomitants of military bases and necessary maneuvers. Among the myriads of absurd accusations were such as these: (1) the Japanese police force had become the " catspaw of America; " (2) the main purpose of the security forces being stationed in Japan was to make certain that a puppet pro-American government like Yoshida's would remain in power; (3) the United States was transforming Japan into a " colony of the United States; " (4) even in the procurement orders for the security forces and for the United Nations troops in Korea the United States was " sweating Japanese labor and industry " by compelling Japanese suppliers to accept orders at " below cost figures."[2]

The solid core of the Japanese citizenry in general did not take these accusations seriously, and most Japanese probably recognized that whatever evils existed as a result of the presence of security forces were inevitable because of the nature of the problem. (Not to recognize the good sense of most Japanese would be a serious omission.) Nevertheless, accusations were being made with reckless abandon, and the Japanese press as a whole could not be called particularly friendly to the United States. It would be absurd and naïve not to recognize that " wild tales " were being cleverly disseminated throughout Japan, that a considerable and dangerous amount of anti-Americanism had come into existence, and that it was probably increasing as a result of the persistent activities and efforts of irresponsible extremists and misguided intellectuals.

THE PROBLEM OF EXTRATERRITORIALITY

The stationing of large numbers of security forces in Japan necessitated the securing of temporary extraterritorial rights for them. These rights, included in an administrative agreement between the United States and Japan, exempted the security forces from the laws and judicial procedure of Japan and entitled them to trial and punishment under the American military code. In actual practice the security forces did not abuse these privileges, and in fact in many instances security force personnel received sterner treatment under the American military code than they would have received under Japanese law and procedure. Nevertheless, the existence of these privileges gave irresponsible extremists an undeserved opportunity to engage in the fruitful concoction of half-truths and outright fabrications for the purpose of creating the impression that Japan is in a colonial or semi-colonial status and of inciting the Japanese public against alleged American imperialism.

Extraterritoriality now has a particularly offensive and humiliating ring to Asia, which invariably associates it with the immoral imperialism and colonialism of the nineteenth century. This is especially true of contemporary Japan, where sensitiveness, always great, is probably now at its most delicate extreme. It was clearly recognized by the State Department that the extraterritorial privileges required some modification if Japanese-American relations were to be placed on a sound basis and if they were to be given the opportunity of attaining the cordiality that is so vitally necessary. Negotiations to this effect were initiated in the summer of 1953, and on September 29 the administrative agreement was revised to eliminate the extraterritorial privileges that had been accorded American military personnel and to place them under Japanese court jurisdiction. The agreement became effective on October 29, and there was good reason to believe it would work out satisfactorily.

THE PROBLEM OF REARMAMENT

Since the outbreak of the Korean War in late June 1950, the United States persistently encouraged Japan to take steps to rearm herself effectively for defense. This the United States did because of the dictates of cold reality and the gravely changed international situation. Communism was running amuck and the Soviet Union had clearly demonstrated that it was the conniving power behind the postwar aggressions that had taken place. Consequently, for the United States the primary problem was the containment of Russian power and Communist aggression.[3] To this end the United States subordinated other problems. For Japan, however, the primary problem was economic survival, the core of which was a large necessary increase of exports so that imports could be balanced. To most Japanese the Russian and Communist threats appeared to be more academic than real. Dependent on the United States, Japan reluctantly found herself compelled to subordinate her economic problem to the American viewpoint that " containment " deserved the highest priority. Although the Yoshida government appeared determined to maintain close relations with the United States, it nevertheless hesitated to antagonize Red China or the Soviet Union. It was obvious that the pro-American Yoshida government was not burning its bridges as far as the future potential trade with Red China, or even with Soviet Russia, was concerned. Even the Yoshida government was unwilling to compromise irretrievably the potential China trade.

While the Yoshida government dealt cautiously with China, and also with Russia, it nevertheless did not hesitate to go forward with the prudent rearmament of Japan. By 1953 a National Safety Force of some 110,000 men and a Coastal Safety Force of about 8,000 men had been established. Although these forces were euphemistically called " safety forces " and " security forces " there was absolutely no question of their being the nucleus of a genuine army and navy, with an airforce clearly in the offing. These forces had been built up cautiously with the encouragement and assistance of the United States, and although the Yoshida government was severely and viciously criticized by extreme Leftist elements it parried and ignored that criticism. Hence, while the Yoshida government was unwilling to write off the potential trade with Red China, it at the same time was not blind to the realities of the time and was determined to take every feasible step toward ensuring the security of Japan against potential external aggressors.

The solid Japanese citizenry, which had been genuinely converted to pacifism by the horrors of war that had been unleashed on the homeland and by the persistent peace indoctrination of the occupation authorities, was somewhat confused by the " silent " growth of an armed force in the face of a solemn constitution which specifically prohibited Japan from maintaining armed forces or from ever availing herself of the right of belligerency. The extremists attempted to exploit this widespread peace conviction and the constitutional prohibition, but the solid mass fatalistically accepted the " silent " rearmament as a necessary evil and apparently placed its trust in the judgment and wisdom of Yoshida.

Although the United States did not apply pressure on Japan to secure her adherence to the critically important policy of containment, it was evident that the United States did apply considerable persuasion and did not hesitate to make its wishes known to the Yoshida government. The irresponsible Leftist elements, as was to be expected, attempted to make political capital of the situation and continuously stigmatized the Yoshida government as a puppet American regime which was transforming Japan into a gigantic military base and unnecessarily provoking Soviet Russia and Red China. The solid mass of the Japanese citizenry did not appear to share this judgment, however, for in the critical elections of April 1953 the Yoshida party was somewhat vindicated at the polls.

In the summer of 1953 the United States outrightly offered Japan M.S.A. (Mutual Security Aid), with the public announcement that the offer was Japan's to accept or reject voluntarily as a sovereign nation. The proferred aid reputedly amounted to well over 100 million dollars for the first year. By this time the Yoshida government had become bolder, and discussions on the practical details of the aid offer were promptly initiated at the Japanese Foreign Office with officials of the American Embassy. Although it was clearly apparent that only a minority of the Japanese public opposed participation in M.S.A., the Socialists raised strong objections and prepared to fight the issue down the line. As negotiations progressed, it became evident that the amount of the aid offered by the United States would be dependent on the degree to which Japan expanded her armed establishment and the contribution which she herself would make to its expansion. Early in September it was disclosed that the Japanese Government was considering a plan which provided for a five-year build-up of the National Safety Force to a total strength of 210,000 men, a sea unit strength of 140,000 gross tons of warships, and an airforce of 1,400 planes.

THE PROBLEM OF ECONOMIC SURVIVAL

It is perhaps no exaggeration to contend that the course which Japanese-American relations will take in the future will depend largely on the course which the Japanese economy will take. That is to say, if Japan's " free " economy can continue to prosper reasonably and meet the basic living requirements of the Japanese people, then Japanese-American relations should remain on a cordial basis and possibly become even more cordial. However, if Japan's " free " economy cannot meet the basic living requirements of the Japanese people, then one can almost be certain that the extremists will gain control of the government and that relations between the United States and Japan will deteriorate rapidly and probably in the end be characterized by open friction and hostility.

As has been indicated, the new Japan under the guiding hand of Prime Minister Yoshida has shown more than a mere token willingness to cooperate with the United States within the framework of basic American world and Far Eastern policy, often to the partial detriment of Japan. For example, the Yoshida government has shunned the strong temptation to " do business " with Red China on a large scale despite the fact that China and Japan are at present natural trading countries and will probably remain so for another generation or two, if not longer. This self-denial was obviously accepted by the Yoshida government for two main reasons: (1) a genuine fear and distrust of Communism and Communist state power as represented by Soviet Russia and Red China; and (2) a feeling, and strong hope, that temporary sacrifices by Japan would be fully, or nearly fully, compensated for by economic assistance from the United States and American help for the Japanese economy in the form of enlightened trade policies.

Any attempt to predict the course of future events, of course, is risky and moreover pointless, as there are too many variables and intangibles involved which have a bearing on the future of Japanese-American relations. However, one prediction can safely be made. If Japan does not have free and equal access to sources of raw materials and markets, the Japanese economy will collapse and the country may become confronted with the most serious economic crisis in its history. One should never lose sight of the fact that Japan has a vast population of some eighty seven millions densely crowded on mountainous islands of less than 150,000 square miles, poor in minerals and with an arable area of less than 16 percent of the total. This huge population is twenty three millions more than it was in 1930, and is currently increasing at the rate of well over a million each year. If peace comes to the world and a world-wide depression takes place, and if with it the United States and other " have " nations again resort to ruthlessly high tariffs and crushing trade restrictions, then one can almost be certain that pro-American orientation will collapse like a house of cards. One can be equally certain in such a case that either the extreme Left or the extreme Right will successfully exploit the widespread misery and discontent and seize power with their promises of better days ahead if the nation will definitely turn its back on the policy of cooperation with the United States and whole-heartedly support their radical and chauvinistic policies.

No people, least of all the Japanese, will remain supine while their industries come to a halt, their wharves become silent, and the shadow of economic distress, suffering and hunger creeps over the land. While it is beyond the province of this study to go into a discussion of the nature of Japan's economy and its critical problems, the point must nevertheless be stressed that Japan's economic future is dark, very dark, and almost but not quite hopeless. This is an unpleasant fact that must be squarely faced, particularly by Americans and their government. The United States cannot, of course, be expected to assume responsibility for the huge and teeming Japanese population, or for the smallness of the Japanese islands and their paucity of resources. Neither can the United States be expected to compensate Japan for the loss of its once rich and far-flung empire. The United States obviously could not be expected to assume these responsibilities or make these compensations because it simply does not have the means to do so. However, the United States can, and must, make certain small and perhaps temporary sacrifices and adopt trade and general cosmopolitan policies which among other things will continually encourage the flow of imports and exports among all free countries. Only by such sacrifices and policies can the United States do its urgently required part to give the Japanese " free " economy a fighting chance for survival.

In particular, Japanese products; those few products which Japan has to offer for export, must be encouraged as well as permitted to find their natural market in the United States, if one actually exists. These products must also be encouraged and permitted to find their natural markets in all other free countries. Undoubtedly, such an enlightened American trade policy will incur the wrath of certain minor producers at home, but the American leaders of state, in the legislature as well as in the executive, have the solemn obligation of living up to the ideals which the United States has been preaching for the past two decades and of equating the long-term welfare of some 160 million Americans against the temporary hardships that may be imposed on a very small and minor segment of the vast American economy : that is to say, the small segment which might suffer from a heavy flow of Japanese exports such as canned fish, silk scarves and pottery. Actually the capital and labor which would be displaced by a such a flow of Japanese exports would soon be re-employed in other industries more natural to the highly industrialized economy of the United States. In turn these industries would doubtless increase their exports to Japan. Admittedly, this is the free-trade argument, but it has not yet been given a fair chance in our times. No one knows what blessings might flow to all men of good will were it put into practice, but regardless of pious wishing, the time has come when the free world must adopt it or repudiate the ideals for which so much blood has been spilled in recent years.

Actually, the United States has no alternative but to make the necessary small sacrifices and to adopt as basic policy the continuous encouragement of unrestricted world trade. It has no alternative if its ideals have not been misunderstood, if it has meant what it has said about aggression being evil and about nations having to live in peace with each other. The alternative is the breakdown of the faith of other nations in the possibility or desirability of permanent peace and the maintenance of the present territorial and administrative status quo. When this faith breaks down there will surely be more wars and more ordeals of blood and human suffering, let alone the utter wastage of billions and billions of dollars of material goods.

Japan did not suddenly spring to life with the arrival of General MacArthur in September 1945. Japan has had a long history, much longer than that of the United States, and longer even that that of any present Western European state. Through their hard work, sacrifices, and particular abilities the Japanese succeeded in fashioning the strongest state in Asia. For nearly half a century Japan stood forth as the equal of any Western power. By following their militarists and ultranationalists the Japanese succeeded in building a rich and powerful empire, with which they enjoyed by far the highest standard of living in Asia and the promise of it continuing to increase. That empire and that standard of living were obtained by denouncing solemn treaties and resorting to wars and aggression. When and if the truly dark and difficult days descend on Japan, that empire will serve as a tempting reminder of the material riches that can be obtained if a nation will but make the temporary sacrifices and support a warlike government which does not hesitate to employ arms against its neighbors. The new world order which all of us of truly democratic leanings hope for and work for must demonstrate to the Japanese people, by deeds, that there is another way to survive, live and prosper. And the United States, the most richly endowed of all the free countries and its leader by choice as well as destiny, must take the initiative in effectively demonstrating to the Japanese that it is to their advantage to be and remain a part of a free, unified, peaceful, one-world trading area.

The Japanese people are not by nature a defeatist people.

Although crushed in the great Pacific War and humbled by a long occupation, Japan has arisen from the ashes of total defeat and again stands forth as the busiest and most highly industrialized nation of Asia. The third Tokyo, that amazing metropolis of steel and concrete which has arisen from the ashes and rubble of World War II, is symbolic of the dream of new Japan: belief in a future with work for all and reasonable security from want and fear. By nature the Japanese instinctively believe in and work for a future. Either the United States will help them find this future of a decent standard of living and reasonable economic security within the framework of world peace and continued cooperation with the United States, or Japan will ultimately take her own road. That road might conceivably lead to Communism and integration of the Japanese economy in a Communist-world, planned-trading area, or it might lead the Japanese people to a detour where the trumpet calls of the ultranationalists and militarists might lure them on a long hike over a trail like the one which led to Pearl Harbor.

REFERENCES

APPENDIXES

SELECTED BIBLIOGRAPHY

INDEX

REFERENCES

CHAPTER I. THE ESTABLISHMENT OF TREATY RELATIONS

1 Shunzo Sakamaki, *Japan and the United States*, 1790–1853, in " Transactions of the Asiatic Society of Japan " (Tokyo, Asiatic Society of Japan, 1939), Second Series, Vol. XVIII, p. 4.
2 Tyler Dennett, *Americans in Eastern Asia* (New York, Macmillan, 1922), p. 242.
3 Sakamaki, *op. cit.*, pp. 150–151.
4 *Cf.* Dennett, *op. cit.*, p. 248.
5 House Doc. 138 : 28–2.
6 John W. Foster, *American Diplomacy in the Orient* (Boston, Houghton Mifflin, 1903), p. 36.
7 Roy Hidemachi Akagi, *Japan's Foreign Relations, 1542–1936* (Tokyo, Hokuseido Press, 1937), p. 20.
8 Cited by Dennett, *op. cit.*, p. 408.
9 Dennett, *op. cit.*, pp. 262–264.

CHAPTER II. THE CRITICAL TRANSITION PERIOD

1 Foster, *op. cit.*, pp. 172–173.
2 Payson J. Treat, *Japan and the United States, 1853–1928* (Stanford, Stanford University Press, 1928), p. 33.
3 Citations from Harris' journal are as recorded in Mario Emilio Cosenza's *The Complete Journal of Townsend Harris* (Garden City, Doubleday Doran 1903).
4 Foster, *op. cit.*, pp. 173–175.
5 *Cf.* Foster, *op. cit.*, pp. 173–174.
6 Carl Crow, *He Opened the Door of Japan* (New York and London, Harper and Brothers. 1939), p. 170.
7 Treat, *op. cit.*, p. 35.
8 Akagi, *op. cit.*, p. 35.
9 Foster, *op. cit.*, p. 184.

10 *Cf.* Dennett, *op. cit.*, p. 412.

11 *Cf. ibid.*, pp. 412–413.

12 Historical Archives Section, Mombusho, *Ishin-shi* (Tokyo, Meiji Shoin, 1940), Vol. 2. pp. 919–933.

13 Treat, *op. cit.*, p. 49.

14 *Cf*, John Bassett Moore, *A Digest of International Law* (Washington, U. S. Govt. Printing Office, 1906), Vol. V. pp. 747–748.

15 Akagi, *op. cit.*, p. 40.

16 George B, Sansom, *The Western World and Japan* (New York, Alfred A. Knopf, 1950), p. 300.

17 *Loc. cit.*

CHAPTER III.   A LONG PERIOD OF CORDIAL RELATIONS

1 Akagi, *op. cit.* p., 52.

2 *Ibid.*, pp. 52–53.

3 *Ibid.*, p. 86.

4 Treat, *op. cit.*, p. 119.

5 *Ibid.*, p. 120.

6 Most of this subchapter discussion is based on an article by the author, " The Korean Problem in the Nineteenth Century " which appeared in the *Monumenta Nipponica* (Tokyo, Sophia University, 1952), Vol. VII.

7 W. W. McLaren, *A Political History of Japan During the Meiji Era*, 1867–1912 (London, Allen and Unwin and New York, Scribners, 1916), p. 35.

8 Henry Satoh, *Lord Hotta, the Pioneer Diplomat of Japan*, cited in Dennett, *op. cit.*, p. 427.

9 Cited by Dennett, *op. cit.*, p. 430.

10 Dennett, *op. cit.*, pp. 432–433.

11 *Ibid.*, p. 498.

12 *Ibid.*, p. 498.

13 *Cf. ibid.*, p. 499.

14 Treat, *op. cit.*, pp. 158–160.

CHAPTER IV.   THE BEGINNINGS OF MISUNDER-STANDINGS AND DIPLOMATIC STRIFE

1 From the text of the Russian note cited in Shigenobu Okuma, *Fifty Years of New Japan* (London, Smith and Elder, 1909), Vol. I, p. 112.

2   Cited by Foster Rhea Dulles, *China and America* (Princeton, Princeton Univercity Press, 1946), p. 112.
3   Cited by Dulles, *op. cit.*, pp. 123–126.
4   A. Whitney Griswold, *The Far Eastern Policy of the United States* (New York, Harcourt, 1938), p. 104.
5   *Cf. ibid.*, pp. 94–96.
6   *Ibid.*, p. 105.
7   Treat, *op. cit.*, p. 205.
8   *Ibid.*, p. 205.
9   *Ibid.*, p. 274.
10 *Ibid.*, p. 275.
11 Cited by Allan Nevins, *Henry White* (New York, Harper and Brothers, 1939), pp. 292–293.
12 William Howard Taft, in annual message to the Congress, December 3, 1912.
13 *Cf.* Griswold, *op. cit.*, p. 157.
14 *U. S. Foreign Relations*, 1910, pp. 234–235.
15 Griswold, *op. cit.*, p. 132.
16 *U.S. Foreign Relations*, 1915, pp. 105–111.
17 *Ibid.*, p. 146.
18 *Cf.* Harold M. Vinacke, *A History of the Far East in Modern Times* (New York, Crofts, 1945), p. 182.
19 *U.S. Foreign Relations, 1917*, p. 264.
20 *U. S. Foreign Relations, 1918, Russia*, Vol. II, p. 288.
21 *Ibid.*, p. 289.

CHAPTER V.   THE WASHINGTON CONFERENCE AND THE QUEST FOR SECURITY

1   Data on the Washington Conference are principally from Raymond Leslie Buell, *The Washington Conference* (New York, Appleton, 1923).
2   George T. Davis, *A Navy Second to None* (New York, Harcourt, Brace, 1940), p. 408.
3   Dept. of State, *The General Pact for the Renunciation of War*, p. 36.
4   Speech of Secretary of State Henry L. Stimson, cited in Dept. of State, *The Pact of Paris—Three Years of Development* (Washington, U.S. Govt. Printing Office 1932).
5   Davis, *op. cit.*, pp. 364–365.

CHAPTER VI. THE FATEFUL DECADE, 1931–1941

1 *U.S. Foreign Relations, Japan, 1931–1941*, Vol. I, pp. 5–7.
2 *Ibid.*, pp. 11–12.
3 *Ibid.*, p. 76.
4 *Ibid.*, pp. 76–77.
5 Dept. of State, *Peace and War, United States Foreign Policy, 1931–1941*, p. 6.
6 *Ibid.*, p. 7.
7 *Ibid.*, p. 7.
8 *U.S. Foreign Relations*, 1931–1941, *Japan*, Vol. I, pp. 127–128.
9 *Ibid.*, pp. 128–129.
10 *Ibid.*, pp. 233–236.
11 *Ibid.*, pp. 240–241.
12 *Ibid.*, pp. 135–143.
13 *Ibid.*, pp. 143–144.
14 *Ibid.*, pp. 149–150.
15 *Ibid.*
16 *International Military Tribunal for the Far East Record*, hereinafter referred to as IMTFE (published in mimeographed form in Tokyo, 1946–1948, by the IMTFE Secretariat), p. 49,295.
17 *Ibid.*, p. 49,297.
18 *U.S. Foreign Relations, Japan, 1931–1941*, Vol. I, pp. 330–333.
19 *Ibid.*, pp. 339–341.
20 *Ibid.*, pp. 355–357.
21 *Ibid.*, pp. 375–377.
22 *Ibid.*, pp. 498–499.
23 *Ibid.*, pp. 504–505.
24 *Ibid.*, p. 506.
25 *Ibid.*, pp. 506–507.
26 *Ibid.*, pp. 384–394.
27 *Ibid.*, pp. 379–382.
28 *Ibid.*, p. 403.
29 *Ibid.*, pp. 417–422.
30 *Ibid.*, pp. 523–524.
31 *Ibid.*, pp. 785–790.
32 *Ibid.*, pp. 797–800.
33 *Ibid.*, pp. 820–826.
34 *U.S. Foreign Relations, Japan, 1931–1941*, Vol. II, p. 281.

35 *Ibid.*, pp. 281–282.

36 *Ibid.*, pp. 420–425.

37 IMTFE, pp. 10,140–10,148.

38 *Ibid.*, pp. 10,188–10,196.

39 *U.S. Foreign Relations, Japan, 1931–1941*, Vol. II, pp. 315–317.

40 *Ibid.*, pp. 608–609.

41 IMTFE, Exhibit 1107, pp. 10,216–10,218.

42 Review of *Thirty-Five Years of Bubbles* by Saburo Kurusu, in the *Nippon Times* (Tokyo), March 29, 1949.

43 IMTFE, p. 10,339.

44 *Ibid.*, p. 10,354.

45 *U.S. Foreign Relations, Japan, 1931–1941*, Vol. II, pp. 752-756.

46 *Cf.* testimony of James Ballantine at the Tokyo war-crime trials, in IMTFE, pp. 10,710–11,165.

47 *U.S. Foreign Relations, Japan, 1931–1941*, Vol. II, pp. 764–770.

48 IMTFE, p. 10,418.

49 *Ibid.*, pp. 10,421–10,426.

50 *U.S. Foreign Relations., Japan, 1931–1941*, Vol. II, pp. 784–786.

51 IMTFE, p. 10,519.

52 *Ibid.*, Exhibit 1218, pp. 10,536–10,537.

53 *U.S. Foreign Relations, Japan, 1931–1941*, Vol. II, pp. 787–792.

54 Dept. of State, *Peace and War, United States Foreign Policy, 1931–1941*, p. 143.

CHAPTER VII.   THE GREAT PACIFIC WAR

1 *Cf.* James F. Byrnes, *Speaking Frankly* (New York, Harper Brothers, 1947), p. 45.

2 *The Axis in Defeat* (Dept. of State, Publication 2433, undated), pp. 29–32.

3 *Ibid.*, pp. 33–38.

CHAPTER VIII.   THE OCCUPATION OF JAPAN

1 *The Axis in Defeat, op. cit.*, pp. 106–107.

2 "United States Initial Post-Surrender Policy for Japan," August 29, 1945; complete text printed in *Occupation of Japan, Policy and Progress* (Dept. of State, Publication 2671, Far Eastern Series 17), Appendix 13, pp. 73–81.

3 "Authority of General MacArthur as Supreme Commander for the Allied Powers," September 6, 1945; in *ibid.*, Appendix 16, pp. 88–89.

4   *Cf.* Dept. of State, Pub. 4392, *Conference for the Conclusion and Signature of the Treaty of Peace with Japan* (Washington, U.S. Govt. Printing Office, 1951), pp. 31–37.

5   *Cf. ibid.,* pp. 102–122.

6   *Cf. ibid.,* pp. 277–281.

7   " Security Treaty, signed September 8, 1951," (issued in mimeographed form by the American Embassy, Tokyo).

8   " Administrative Agreement under Article III of the Security Treaty," (issued in mimeographed form by the American Embassy, Tokyo).

CHAPTER IX.   SOVEREIGN JAPAN AND THE FUTURE

1   These typical stock accusations were advanced by a Japanese intellectual at a round-table conference held in Tokyo, in June 1953, which was concerned with a discussion of anti-Americanism in Japan. (*Cf. Tokyo Evening News,* June 6, 1953).

2   The author became intimately familiar with these wild accusations while engaged in a research project in the spring of 1953 which concentrated on the Tokyo, Osaka, Kyoto and Kobe areas.

3   This aspect of conflict between Japanese and American post-treaty policies is ably discussed by Edwin O. Reischauer in *Japan and America : Political Issues* (New York, Institute of Pacific Relations, 1953).

Appendix 1

AMERICAN SECRETARIES OF STATE

	Date appointed	President
Thomas Jefferson	Mar. 22, 1790	Washington
Edmund Randolph	Jan. 2, 1794	Washington
Timothy Pickering	Dec. 10, 1795	Washington; John Adams
John Marshall	June 6, 1800	John Adams
James Madison	May 2, 1801	Jefferson
Robert Smith	Mar. 6, 1809	Madison
James Monroe	Apr. 6, 1811	Madison
John Quincy Adams	Sep. 22, 1817	Monroe
Henry Clay	Mar. 7, 1825	John Q. Adams
Martin Van Buren	Mar. 28, 1829	Jackson
Edward Livingston	May 24, 1831	Jackson
Louis McLane	May 29, 1833	Jackson
John Forsyth	July 1, 1834	Jackson; Van Buren
Daniel Webster	Mar. 6, 1841	Harrison; Tyler
Abel P. Upshur	July 24, 1843	Tyler
John C. Calhoun	Apr. 1, 1844	Tyler
James Buchanan	Mar. 10, 1845	Polk
John M. Clayton	Mar. 8, 1849	Taylor
Daniel Webster	July 23, 1850	Fillmore
Edward Everett	Nov. 6, 1852	Fillmore
William L. Marcy	Mar. 8, 1853	Pierce
Lewis Cass	Mar. 6, 1857	Buchanan
Jeremiah S. Black	Dec. 17, 1860	Buchanan
William H. Seward	Mar. 6, 1861	Lincoln; Johnson
Elihu B. Washburne	Mar. 5, 1869	Grant
Hamilton Fish	Mar. 17, 1869	Grant
William M. Evarts	Mar. 12, 1877	Hayes
James G. Blaine	Mar. 7, 1881	Garfield; Arthur
Frederick T. Frelinghuysen	Mar. 6, 1885	Arthur
Thomas F. Bayard	Mar. 7, 1885	Cleveland
James G. Blaine	Mar. 7, 1889	Harrison

	Date Appointed	President
John W. Foster	June 29, 1892	Harrison
Walter Q. Gresham	Mar. 7, 1893	Cleveland
Richard Olney	June 10, 1895	Cleveland
John Sherman	Mar. 6, 1897	McKinley
William R. Day	Apr. 28, 1898	McKinley
John Hay	Sep. 30, 1898	McKinley; Roosevelt
Elihu Root	July 19, 1905	Roosevelt
Robert Bacon	Jan. 27, 1909	Roosevelt
Philander C. Knox	Mar. 6, 1909	Taft
William Jennings Bryan	Mar. 5, 1913	Wilson
Robert Lansing	June 24, 1915	Wilson
Bainbridge Colby	Mar. 23, 1920	Wilson
Charles E. Hughes	Mar. 5, 1921	Harding; Coolidge
Frank B. Kellogg	Mar. 5, 1925	Coolidge
Henry L. Stimson	Mar. 28, 1929	Hoover
Cordell Hull	Mar. 4, 1933	Hoover
Edward R. Stettinius, Jr.	Dec. 1, 1944	Roosevelt; Truman
James F. Byrnes	July 3, 1945	Truman
George E. Marshall	Jan. 21, 1947	Truman
Dean Acheson	Jan. 19, 1949	Truman
John Foster Dulles	Jan. 21, 1953	Eisenhower

Appendix 2

JAPANESE FOREIGN MINISTERS

	Date appointed		Date appointed
Kaoru Inoue	Dec. 23, 1885	Hikokichi Ijūin	Sep. 19, 1923
Hirobumi Itō	Sep. 17, 1887	Keishirō Matsui	Jan. 7, 1924
Shigenobu Ōkuma	Feb. 1, 1888	Kijūrō Shidehara	June 11, 1924
Shūzō Aoki	Dec. 24, 1889	Giichi Tanaka	Apr. 10, 1927
Takeaki Enomoto	May 29, 1891	Kijūrō Shidehara	July 2, 1929
Munemitsu Mutsu	Aug. 8, 1892	Tsuyoshi Inukai	Dec. 13, 1931
Kinmochi Saionji	June 5, 1895	Kenkichi Yoshizawa	Jan. 14, 1932
Shigenobu Ōkuma	Sep. 22, 1896	Makoto Saitō	May 26, 1932
Tokujirō Nishi	Nov. 6, 1897	Yasuya Uchida	July 7, 1932
Shigenobu Ōkuma	June 30, 1898	Kōki Hirota	Sep. 14 1933
Shūzō Aoki	Nov. 8, 1898	Hachirō Arita	Apr. 2, 1936
Kōmei Katō	Oct. 19, 1900	Senjūrō Hayashi	Feb. 2, 1937
Arasuke Sone	June 2, 1901	Naotake Satō	Mar. 3, 1937
Jutarō Komura	Sep. 21, 1901	Kōki Hirota	June 4, 1937
Tarō Katsura	July 3, 1905	Kazushige Ugaki	May 26, 1938
Kōmei Katō	Jan. 7, 1906	Fumimaro Konoe	Sep. 30, 1938
Kinmochi Saionji	Mar. 3, 1906	Hachirō Arita	Oct. 29, 1938
Tadasu Hayashi	May 19, 1906	Nobuyuki Abe	Aug. 30, 1939
Masakata Terauchi	July 14, 1908	Kichisaburō Nomura	Sep. 25, 1939
Jutarō Komura	Aug. 27, 1908	Hachirō Arita	Jan. 16, 1940
Tadasu Hayashi	Aug. 30, 1911	Yōsuke Matsuoka	July 22, 1940
Yasuya Uchida	Oct. 6, 1911	Teijirō Toyoda	July 18, 1941
Tarō Katsura	Dec. 12, 1912	Shigenori Tōgō	Oct. 18, 1941
Kōmei Katō	Jan. 29, 1913	Hideki Tōjō	Sep. 1, 1942
Nobuaki Makino	Feb. 20, 1913	Masayuki Tani	Sep. 17, 1942
Kōmei Katō	Apr. 16, 1914	Mamoru Shigemitsu	Apr. 20, 1943
Shigenobu Ōkuma	Aug. 10, 1915	Kantarō Suzuki	Apr. 7, 1945
Kikujirō Ishii	Oct. 13, 1915	Shigenori Tōgō	Apr. 9, 1945
Masakata Terauchi	Oct. 9, 1916	Mamoru Shigemitsu	Aug. 17, 1945
Ichirō Motono	Nov. 21, 1916	Shigeru Yoshida	Sep. 17, 1945
Shimpei Gotō	Apr. 23, 1918	Hitoshi Ashida	Jan. 1, 1947
Yasuya Uchida	Sep. 29, 1918	Shigeru Yoshida	Oct. 19, 1948
Gonnohyōe Yamamoto	Sep. 2, 1923	Katsuo Okazaki	Apr. 30, 1952

Appendix 3

AMERICAN DIPLOMATIC REPRESENTATIVES TO JAPAN

	Date	Title
Townsend Harris (New York)	Jan. 19, 1859	Minister Resident
Robert H. Pruyn (New York)	Oct. 12, 1861	,, ,,
Robert B. Van Valkenburgh (New York)	Jan. 18, 1866	,, ,,
Charles E. De Long (Nevada)	Apr. 21, 1869	,, ,,
	Jul. 14, 1870	Envoy Extraordinary
John A. Bingham (Ohio)	May 31, 1873	,, ,,
Richard B. Hubbard (Texas)	Apr. 2, 1885	,, ,,
John F. Swift (Calif.)	Mar. 12, 1889	,, ,,
Frank L. Coombs (Calif.)	Apr. 20, 1892	,, ,,
Edwin Dun (Ohio)	Apr. 4, 1893	,, ,,
Alfred E. Buck (Georgia)	Apr. 13, 1897	,, ,,
Lloyd C. Griscom (Penna.)	Dec. 16, 1902	,, ,,
Luke E. Wright (Tenn.)	Jan. 25, 1906	Amb. Extr. & Plenip.
Thomas J. O'Brien (Mich.)	June 11, 1907	,, ,,
Charles Page Bryan (Illinois)	Aug. 12, 1911	,, ,,
Larz Anderson (Dist. of Columbia)	Nov. 14, 1912	,, ,,
George W. Guthrie (Penna.)	May 20, 1913	,, ,,
Roland S. Morris (Penna.)	Aug. 1, 1917	,, ,,
Charles Beecher Warren (Mich.)	June 29, 1921	,, ,,
Cyrus E. Woods (Penna.)	Mar. 3, 1923	,, ,,
Edgar A. Bancroft (Illinois)	Sep. 23, 1924	,, ,,
Charles MacVeagh (N.H.)	Sep. 24, 1925	,, ,,
William R. Castle (Dist. of Columbia)	Dec. 11, 1929	,, ,,
W. Cameron Forbes (Mass.)	June 17, 1930	,, ,,
Joseph C. Grew (N.H.)	Feb. 19, 1932	,, ,,
George Atcheson. Jr. (Calif.)	Sep. 7, 1945	Ambassador*
William J. Sebald (Maryland)	Jan. 7, 1949	Minister*
Robert D. Murphy (Wis.)	Apr. 21, 1952	Amb. Extr. & Plenip.
John M. Allison (Kan.)	Apr. 8, 1953	,, ,,

* Served as Political Adviser to the Supreme Commander for the Allied Powers.

Appendix 4

JAPANESE DIPLOMATIC REPRESENTATIVES TO THE UNITED STATES

	Date	*Title*
Arinori Mori	Oct. 5, 1870	Minister
Kagenori Ueno	Oct. 20, 1872	Minister Resident
Kiyonori Yoshida	Nov. 9, 1874	Envoy Extraordinary and Min. Plenip.
Munenori Terajima	Oct. 28, 1882	,, ,, ,, ,, ,,
Ryūichi Kuki	Sep. 14, 1884	,, ,, ,, ,, ,,
Munemitsu Mutsu	June 11, 1888	,, ,, ,, ,, ,,
Kyōzō Takeno	Jan. 24, 1891	,, ,, ,, ,, ,,
Shin-ichirō Kurino	Aug. 6, 1894	,, ,, ,, ,, ,,
Tōru Hoshi	Jun. 24, 1896	,, ,, ,, ,, ,,
Jutarō Komura	Nov. 20, 1898	,, ,, ,, ,, ,,
Kogorō Takahira	July 31, 1900	,, ,, ,, ,, ,,
Shūzō Aoki	Apr. 24, 1906	Ambassador Extraordinary and Plenip.
Kogorō Takahira	Feb. 3, 1908	,, ,, ,, ,,
Yasuya Uchida	Dec. 23, 1909	,, ,, ,, ,,
Sutemi Chinda	Feb. 22, 1912	,, ,, ,, ,,
Yoshimaro Satō	Oct. 9, 1916	,, ,, ,, ,,
Kikujirō Ishii	Aprl 26, 1918	,, ,, ,, ,,
Kijūrō Shidehara	Nov. 1, 1919	,, ,, ,, ,,
Masanao Uehara	Feb. 18, 1923	,, ,, ,, ,,
Tsuneo Matsudaira	Mar. 11, 1925	,, ,, ,, ,,
Katsuji Debuchi	Oct. 17, 1928	,, ,, ,, ,,
Hiroshi Saitō	Jan. 10, 1934	,, ,, ,, ,,
Kensuke Horiuchi	Dec. 17, 1938	,, ,, ,, ,,
Kichisaburō Nomura	Feb. 11, 1941	,, ,, ,, ,,
Eikichi Araki	June 7, 1952	,, ,, ,, ,,

Note:—The date is for arrival at post.

SELECTED BIBLIOGRAPHY

Abbott, James Francis, *Japanese Expansionism and American Politics* (New York, Macmillan, 1916).

Akagi, Roy Hidemachi, *Japan's Foreign Relations, 1542–1936* (Tokyo, Hokuseido Press, 1937).

Bailey, Thomas A., *Theodore Roosevelt and the Japanese-American Crisis* (Stanford, Stanford University Press, 1934).

Bisson, Thomas A., *American Policy in the Far East: 1931–1940* (New York, Institute of Pacific Relations, 1939).

Buell, Raymond Leslie, *The Washington Conference* (New York, Appleton, 1923).

Clinard, Dutten Jones, *Japan's Influence on American Naval Power, 1897–1917* (Berkeley, University of California Press, 1947).

Cole, Allan B. (ed.), *Yankee Surveyors in the Shogun's Seas* (Princeton, Princeton University Press, 1947).

Cosenza, Mario Emilio (ed.), *The Complete Journal of Townsend Harris* (Garden City, Doubleday Doran, 1930).

Crow, Carl, *He Opened the Door of Japan* (New York and London, Harper and Brothers, 1939).

Dennett, Tyler, *Americans in Eastern Asia* (New York, Macmillan, 1922).

——, *Roosevelt and the Russo-Japanese War* (New York, Macmillan, 1925).

Dept. of State, *Foreign Relations of the United States* (Washington, U.S. Govt. Printing Office: annual publications).

——, *Foreign Relations of the United States, 1931–1941, Japan* (Washington, U.S. Govt. Printing Office, 1943), two volumes.

——, *Peace and War, United States Foreign Relations, 1931–1941* (Washington, U.S. Govt. Printing Office).

——, *Occupation of Japan, Policy and Progress* (Dept. of State Publication 2671, Far Eastern Series 17).

——, *Conference for the Conclusion and Signature of the Treaty of Peace with Japan: Record of Proceedings* (Washington, U.S. Govt. Printing Office).

Dulles, Foster Rhea, *Forty Years of American-Japanese Relations* (New York and London, Appleton-Century, 1937).

Feary, Robert A., *The Occupation of Japan* (New York, Macmillan, 1950): a sequel to Martin's *The Allied Occupation of Japan*.

Feis, Herbert, *The Road to Pearl Harbor* (Princeton, Princeton University Press, 1950).

Foster, John W., *American Diplomacy in the Orient* (Boston, Houghton Mifflin, 1903).

Graves, William S., *America's Siberian Adventure* (New York, Peter Smith, 1931).

Grew, Joseph, *Ten Years in Japan* (New York, Simon and Schuster, 1944).

——, *Turbulent Era* (Boston, Houghton Mifflin, 1952), two volumes.

Griswold, A. Whitney, *The Far Eastern Policy of the United States* (New York, Harcourt, 1938).

Gulick, Sidney L., *Toward Understanding Japan* (New York, Macmillan, 1935).

Hishida, S. G., *The International Position of Japan as a Great Power* (New York, Columbia University Press, 1905).

——, *Japan Among the Great Powers* (New York, Longmans Green, 1940).

Ichihashi, Yamato, *Japanese in the United States* (Stanford, Stanford University Press, 1932).

——, *The Washington Conference and After* (Stanford, Stanford University Press, 1928).

Iyenaga, T. and Kenosuke Sato, *Japan and the California Problem* (New York, G. P. Putnam's Sons, 1921).

Kawakami, Kiyoshi, *American-Japanese Relations* (New York, Macmillan, 1912).

——, *Japan in World Politics* (New York, Macmillan, 1917).

——, *Japan's Pacific Policy* (New York, Macmillan, 1922).

——, *The Real Japanese Question* (New York, Macmillan, 1921).

Latourette, Kenneth Scott, *The American Record in the Far East, 1945–1951* (New York, Macmillan, 1952).

Martin, Edward M., *The Allied Occupation of Japan*: *an Interim Report* (New York, Institute of Pacific Relations, 1948).

Mears, Helen, *Mirror for Americans* (Boston, Houghton Mifflin, 1948).

Moore, Frederick, *With Japan's Leaders* (London, Chapman and Hall,

1943).

Nitobe, Inazo, *The Japanese Nation* (New York, G. P. Putnam's Sons, 1912): pages 258–330 are of interest to a student of Japanese-American relations.

Reischauer, Edwin O., *The United States and Japan* (Cambridge, Harvard University Press, 1950).

Sakamaki, Shunzo, *Japan and the United States*, 1790–1853, printed in "Transactions of the Asiatic Society of Japan" (Tokyo, Asiatic Society of Japan, 1939), Second Series, Vol. XVIII.

Sansom, Sir George, *The Western World and Japan* (New York, Knopf, 1950).

Saito, Hirosi, *Japan's Policies and Purposes* (Boston, Marshall Jones, 1935).

Satow, Sir Ernest, *A Diplomat in Japan* (London, Seeley, Service, 1921).

Tokutomi, Iichiro, *Japanese-American Relations*, translated by Sukeshige Yanagiwara (New York, Macmillan, 1922).

Treat, Payson J., *Japan and the United States, 1853–1928* (Stanford, Stanford University Press, 1928).

Vinacke, Harold M., *The United States and the Far East*, 1945–1951 (Stanford, Stanford University Press, 1952).

Wada, Teijuhn, *American Foreign Policy Towards Japan During the Nineteenth Century* (Tokyo, Toyo Bunko, 1928).

Walforth, Arthur, *Black Ships off Japan* (New York, Knopf, 1946).

Wallach, Sidney (ed.)., *Narrative of the Expedition of an American Squadron to the China Seas and Japan under the Command of Commodore M. C. Perry, United States Navy, Compiled at His Request and under His Supervision, by Francis T. Hawks* (New York, Coward-McCann, 1952).

Wildes, Harry Emerson, *Aliens in the East* (Philadelphia, University of Pennsylvania Press, 1937).

INDEX

Adams, John Quincy, 7
Alcock, Sir Rutherford, 32
Aleutian Islands, 124
Allied Council for Occupied Japan, 139, 140
Anglo-Japanese Treaty of 1894, 42
Anglo-Japanese Alliance, 53
Anti-Americanism in Japan (postwar), 165–166
Anti-foreignism in Japan (Tokugawa period), 29–35
Araki, Eikichi, 164
Arita, Hachiro, 99
Arrow War, 26
Atlantic Charter, 120, 128
Attlee, Clement, 131
Aulick, Commodore, 10
Axis Tripartite Military Pact (1940), 110

Basic Occupation Directive, 141
Biddle, Commodore, 9
Bingham, John A., 40
"Black Ships," 13
Boissonade, Gustave Emile, 39
Bonin Islands, 45, 158, 159, 160, 161
Borah, Senator William E., 76, 81
Borchard, Prof. Edwin, 85
Boxer Rebellion and Protocol, 51–52
Briand, Aristide, 81, 82
British Commonwealth Forces (in occupied Japan), 142
Brussels Conference, 104–105

Bryan, William Jennings, 65, 67, 68
Butler, Nicholas Murray, 81
Byrnes, James, 133

Cairo Conference and Declaration, 124–125, 132
California (discovery of gold), 10
Chang Hsüeh-liang, 90
Changchun, 57
Chiang Kai-shek, 89, 90, 100, 101, 110, 111, 112, 125
China: early relations with Japan, 3–4; early "China trade," 8; rivalry and war with Japan (1894), 46–47; scramble for concessions in, 51; Boxer Rebellion and Protocol, 51–52; Hay Open Door notes concerning, 51, 52, 55–56; "dollar diplomacy" in, 63–65; Twenty-One Demands served on, 66–68; secret treaties affecting, 68; entrance in World War I, 68–69; at the Paris Peace Conference (1919), 71; internal conditions at time of Washington Conference, 77; Manchuria incident with Russia (1929), 84; Japanese invasion of Manchuria, 90; appeal to League of Nations, 92; diplomatic crisis concerning Manchuria, 92–96; Japanese aggression in North China, 96–97; undeclared war with Japan, 101 ff.